New Perspectives in History

The Chinese Revolution: 1900–1950

New Perspectives in History

The Chinese Revolution
1900–1950

Edited by

RANBIR VOHRA

Houghton Mifflin Company • **Boston**

Atlanta • *Dallas* • *Geneva, Illinois* • *Hopewell, New Jersey*
Palo Alto • *London*

Printed in the U.S.A.
Library of Congress Catalog Card Number: 73-14494
ISBN: 0-395-18338-3

Contents

Introduction

Unlike the French Revolution and the Russian Revolution, which have more clearly perceivable time scales, "the Chinese Revolution" is difficult to place in time. Did it begin in the mid-nineteenth century when Western aggression and internal rebellion created a crisis that led inexorably to the breakdown of the traditional order? Or did the revolution start with the overthrow of the Manchu dynasty in 1911? Can we consider the revolution to have concluded in 1949 with the proclamation of the People's Republic of China? Or is it still continuing?

In this collection of readings we have taken the fifty years preceding 1950 as the significant period of the revolution. It was after the defeat of China in the Sino-Japanese War of 1895 and the failure of the Reform Movement in 1898 that the revolution gained real momentum. The collapse of the Ch'ing dynasty was the first step in the revolutionary process that was ultimately to bring basic changes in the political, social, and economic order. The most important part of the story ends in 1949 with the Communist victory which reunified China and gave it a strong nationalist government. The Communists had also developed an ideology and organization that could, at last, effectively replace the traditional system.

In a volume of this size it is impossible to do more than highlight the important phases of the revolutionary process that has wrought so many vast changes. The book incorporates commentaries and analyses by Chinese leaders actually involved in the revolutionary events, as well as analyses by scholars. It is hoped that this will give the student a "feel" of the Chinese experience and help him to comprehend better the meaning and nature of the Chinese Revolution.

The book follows a chronological order but omits political history, which the student should gain elsewhere and constantly bear in mind. Two of the most important elements forming the backdrop to the revolution are: (a) the nature and extent of imperialist activity in China, and (b) the succession of ineffectual Chinese governments which made foreign aggression possible. In this context the nature of the revolution can readily be understood in terms of nationalism (which became increasingly associated with anti-imperialism) and the search for a viable substitute for Confucian ideology and institutions (which led

increasingly to borrowing from Western institutions, ideas, and values).
Thus, political opposition to the Western powers had to be reconciled
with admiration for certain qualities of the West. This naturally
produced an ambivalence in Chinese twentieth-century nationalism until
Communism entered the scene. Chinese Communism "scientifically"
explained the correctness of "anti-imperialist" and "anti-feudal"
stands (warlords and Confucianism were both considered "feudal"),
put China in the forefront of world-historical change, used nationalism
to reassert China's political greatness, and rehabilitated China's image
of its uniqueness.

From the middle of the nineteenth century to the 1940s, the presence
of the imperialist powers was a "permanent" factor in the Chinese
political scene. Humiliated by defeat, bullied into signing unequal
treaties, China was forced to abdicate many of its sovereign rights.
While gunboats in Chinese waters and foreign troops on Chinese soil
made a mockery of Chinese independence and sovereignty, foreign
missionaries and traders traveled with impunity in the Chinese interior
and their activities disturbed the local scene. Foreign powers reduced to
colonial status the countries on China's periphery, which had been
"tributaries" of China, and then went on to divide China into spheres of
interest. The Russo-Japanese War of 1905, the Twenty-one Demands on
China by Japan in 1915, Japanese occupation of Manchuria in 1931, and
finally the Japanese invasion of China in 1937, form the background to
the revolutionary upsurge in China.

Fear of the West is an underlying theme of the revolution, and two
readings—one from K'ang Yu-wei in Section I and the other from Mao
Tse-tung in Section V—show how the coercive policies of the imperialists were scored by Chinese leaders to highlight national weaknesses
and emphasize the need for change. Throughout this period Chinese
intellectuals of all shades of opinion were bound together by a common
aspiration: to see China emerge once again as a strong country,
powerful enough to throw out the foreigner and re-establish its ancient
greatness.

Parallel to the growth of imperialist activity we can trace the growth
of nationalism in China. There were stirrings of early nationalism in a
number of scholar-bureaucrats in the 1890s, including that remarkable
group headed by K'ang Yu-wei, which was soon to call for a spiritual
renewal of the nation. This patriotic awakening spread after 1900 to a
much larger community of the urban elite. Section I gives the background to the 1911 Revolution and shows how the rising sense of

nationalism, which provided the main revolutionary force, was fostered not only by the revolutionaries but by the activities of the reformers and even by the belated reforms introduced by the Ch'ing government.

The failure of the 1911 Revolution as an experiment in the republican form of government was tragically frustrating for many who had enthusiastically hoped for a sudden solution of China's problems. Patriotic thinkers now realized, more than ever before, that social and political issues were intimately connected. The Confucian political system could not be replaced without Confucian culture giving way to new social and ethical values. Section II examines the reasons for the failure of the 1911 Revolution and highlights some of the developments from 1915 to the early 1920s, when intellectuals re-examined Confucian values and culture and tried to find substitutes in Western ideas of nationalism, liberalism, democracy, and science. This was also the time when classical Chinese, the vehicle for Confucianism, was discarded in favor of writing in the vernacular. The birth of modern Chinese literature, the re-evaluation of the past, the heated debates on philosophy and science, and the establishment of new schools of thought justify the use of the terms "literary revolution" and "cultural revolution" to describe developments in this period.

Although the new culture movement had limited success in introducing liberalism and democracy to China, it indicates one important aspect of the Chinese revolution—the need to create a "new" man. At the turn of the century, Liang Ch'i-ch'ao had talked of "renovating the nation" and of "new people." The May Fourth Movement took up this theme more vigorously and released a flood of criticism against the "old and rotten" elements of traditional society. The trend to "remake" Chinese society has continued into the present when scholars discuss "the Maoist vision of a new man."

Until 1911 nationalism was directed against the Manchus rather than the foreigners. It was only after 1911 and particularly after the May Fourth Movement in 1919 that a spirit of protest against the imperialists assumed nationwide proportions. With the reorganization of the Kuomintang (KMT) and the founding of the Chinese Communist Party (CCP), anti-imperialism became a fundamental platform of the revolutionaries.

The theme of Section III is the new high tide of revolution marked by a primary concern with anti-imperialism and a quest for political unification. Modern nationalism can be said to have emerged at last with the May Fourth Incident. At the same time, the success of the Russian

Revolution made Marxism-Leninism relevant to China, and we notice how intellectuals frustrated with the West turned to Communism. Moscow played a leading role in helping to establish the CCP and to reorganize and arm the KMT. But the alliances between the KMT and Russia and between the KMT and the CCP were full of contradictions and lasted only as long as each side had use for the other. Imperialism was their common enemy and national unification their common goal. After the death of Sun Yat-sen in 1925 there was no political leader of his stature to pull the divisive forces together. Russia had hoped to guide the Chinese Revolution but failed tragically in its aim.

In 1927 the right wing of the revolution took over and the left wing was suppressed. Chiang Kai-shek wrested the leadership from civilian hands and made military unification of China the chief goal of the government. All major programs of social change were set aside and compromises were made to gain the support of the conservative landlord class, the warlords, and the rich bankers and merchants. Although this led to immediate success, it also laid the foundation for the KMT's ultimate failure.

From 1927 to 1937, the revolution suffered a setback. It is, however, during this dark period that revolutionary intellectuals turned to the larger problem of politicizing the masses. The activities and thinking of Mao Tse-tung are particularly relevant because his techniques and ideas that had their beginnings during this critical decade were later enshrined in "Maoism" (Section V).

As mentioned earlier the growth of nationalism and the search for a viable social and political system to replace Confucianism went hand in hand. The two-thousand-year-old imperial system had provided China with the world's most durable and stable social and political order. Confucian ideology and institutions had given a unique coherence and unity to Chinese civilization. The political decline that followed the 1911 Revolution only proved the strength of the imperial tradition. For forty years Chinese thinkers and leaders grappled with assessing the worth of the ideas, values, and institutions inherited from the past and those they could borrow from the West. They consciously attacked tradition and rejected it, just as they consciously chose to propagate democracy and liberalism, or later, Marxism-Leninism. In the final analysis we will notice that parliamentary democracy failed to strike roots in China because it was so alien to the Chinese tradition.

Although practically all leading thinkers from K'ang Yu-wei on stressed the need for greater political participation by the people, there was no strong movement to introduce "civil liberties" or government by "majority decision." Indeed, even the liberal thinkers attacked the demand for individual liberties as a demand for self-indulgence. The individual should be prepared to sacrifice himself for the state instead of thinking selfishly of his own benefit. As for "majority decision," it was out of the question. Sun Yat-sen had plans for a period of political tutelage following the military unification of China. Both the KMT and the CCP accepted this basic approach, which emphasized the need for a patriotic, dedicated, and competent elite to head an authoritarian but benevolent political system. The success of Chinese Communism—modern totalitarianism—is partly due to the Chinese political tradition of authoritarianism, centralism, and control.

The social revolution, however, made a far greater break with the past. Apart from changes in attitudes toward the family and the nation, ideas of social revolution ultimately implied the elimination of the vast gap between the educated elite and the illiterate peasantry, which formed the bulk of the population. Patriotic Chinese were aware of the terrible plight of the countryside, and after the May Fourth Incident, many leaders of thought, particularly the Communists, turned their attention to the problems of mass literacy and land reform. For various reasons, the KMT, which depended heavily on the conservative landlord class, could not carry out its rural program. It was left to the CCP and to Mao Tse-tung to experiment with rural reform and in the process mobilize the peasantry and reduce the barriers between city and village, and between intellectual and laborer.

Agricultural crisis was a major internal cause of the disintegration of the traditional social order. Even by 1800, the population of China had grown to the enormous figure of 300 million. This put a great pressure on the land and depressed the living standards of the people. In the nineteenth century, the population rose another 100 million and poverty became endemic in the countryside. Tenancy and rural indebtedness increased, as did the numbers of landless peasants, vagrants, and bandits. The traditional self-sufficiency of the villages was undermined while taxes, rents, and the cost of living kept rising.

Section IV gives a picture of the harsh life of the peasantry in the 1930s. Despite unmitigated suffering from famines, pestilence, and war, it is true that the condition of the peasantry was not an immediate factor leading to the revolution; however, conditions for a revolutionary movement did accummulate in the countryside and the Chinese peasants were ripe for revolution. Without a far-reaching land reform program no revolution could succeed in China. The Kuomintang failed to implement agrarian reforms and win over the peasantry. Where the KMT failed the CCP succeeded.

After 1937, when the Sino-Japanese War broke out, the Kuomintang lost its economic base in the coastal cities and came to rely even more heavily on the landlord class. The military dictatorship of Chiang Kai-shek became increasingly oppressive. Lacking both an ideology that could unify the people and an effective, efficient government that could provide a moral leadership, it lost the support of the intellectuals and the peasantry. Even the KMT armies and bureaucracy became demoralized by the state of affairs.

On the other hand, the war provided the Communists an opportunity to rebuild their shattered party organization, develop their army, and, most important, mobilize peasant support through political propaganda and land reform. Section V emphasizes the reasons for Mao Tse-tung's success and Chiang Kai-shek's failure.

We have refrained from elaborating on Chiang Kai-shek's conservative ideology and from a discussion of the tactics ("United Front," "New Democracy," guerrilla warfare, etc.) employed by the Communists. This volume is intended only to lay the foundation and provide an outline of the great Chinese Revolution. It is hoped that it will encourage some to go on to a more specialized study of the subject.

Ranbir Vohra
Trinity College
Hartford, Connecticut

I Preparation for Revolution

This section deals with the period 1898 to 1911 and shows how China reacted to the humiliating defeat by Japan in 1895 and the sharply increased imperialistic activity that followed in the wake of the war. The selections reveal the deep concern of both the reformers and the revolutionaries for the fate of China. While calling for a spiritual renewal based on native resources they were also searching for Western ideas and institutions that could be borrowed to re-establish the greatness of their country.

The phrase "reform and revolution," which many historians have used in writing about this period, has the unfortunate implication of contrasting opposites. It tends to obscure the fact that the reformers not only aimed at revolutionary changes but were responsible for spreading revolutionary ideas. By highlighting the misuses of authority, the demand for constitutional changes, and the need for social reforms and cultural transformation, the reformers were paving the way for more radical action. The reformers' search for nonviolent change within the framework of the imperial system was greatly weakened by the fact that they had to flee from imperial China and propagate their ideas from exile.

It is understandable why the more radical thinkers—some of whom got their early inspiration from the reformers—would try to defy authority and call for an overthrow of the despotic rulers. It was increasingly felt that the Manchus as alien "barbarians" were bent on suppressing the Chinese and keeping them from fulfilling their legitimate aspirations, so the overthrow of the rulers came to imply the overthrow of the dynasty. The revolutionaries aimed at establishing a United States–type republic which could guarantee democracy and freedom within the framework of a written constitution. This could be achieved only by violence. The irony is that even the reforms introduced by the Ch'ing government after 1900 helped to strengthen the forces of revolution.

K'ANG YU-WEI

The Nation Is in Danger[1]

K'ang Yu-wei (1858–1927) was schooled in the Confucian tradition but he, and other like-minded younger scholars who had been exposed to new ideas from the West, felt that if China did not undertake massive institutional reforms it would disappear as a nation and share the fate of countries like Poland, India, and Burma. With suitable reforms, however, China could acquire military strength and an international status as Russia had done under Peter the Great and Japan under the Meiji Emperor.

In 1898 the Emperor was won over to the idea of political change, and accepting the advice of K'ang Yu-wei and other reformers, he ordered thorough changes in various institutions of government. The Emperor and his idealistic advisers lacked political acumen, and the flood of edicts only resulted in strong opposition from the vast vested interests that they had endangered. The Reform Era lasted only a hundred days, after which the conservative Empress Dowager returned to power, the Emperor was virtually imprisoned, the reformers involved either fled abroad or were arrested and executed, and all the decrees were annulled.

In the following speech made on April 17, 1898, at Peking, K'ang Yu-wei analyzes the reasons for China's failure to defend its sovereignty. Note K'ang's emphasis upon the role of the intellectuals; it is through their will, not that of the common people or even the government, that he believes the country can be saved.

It matters little whether we are rich or poor; we 400 million Chinese are today in serious difficulties. We live in a house which is about to collapse, a boat which, leaking badly, is about to topple over. We are on a pile of firewood which has already caught fire; indeed, our position is no better than that of a bird in a cage, a fish in a frying pan, or a prisoner in a cell. We are treated like slaves; no, we are treated worse than slaves. We are treated like horses and cattle or dogs and sheep that are to be pushed around as our masters please, or cut into pieces

From Dun J. Li, *China in Transition: 1517–1911*, published by Van Nostrand Reinhold Co., copyright 1969 by Litton Educational Publishing, Inc., pp. 229-236. Reprinted by permission.

whenever they choose. This tragedy of enormous proportion is un-precedented in our history, a history that has lasted twenty dynasties or 4,000 years. The decline of our sage's teachings[2] and the impending extermination of the very life of the nation—how can any tragedy be more painful than this one? It is so painful that words are inadequate to describe it.

Since ancient times we Chinese have been proud of the fact that ours is a nation of great achievement. Around us are such small countries as Burma, Korea, Annam, and Liu-ch'iu that we once dominated. We have in fact maintained a sense of superiority for a long time. Because of this sense of superiority, we, at the beginning of the present dynasty [the Ch'ing or Manchu Dynasty], viewed England and France as small island kingdoms in the South China Sea. Even our most informed men of letters . . . did not know much outside the cultural confines of China. . . . The learned scholars of the eighteenth century did not have even the most rudimentary knowledge [regarding countries outside China] which the merchants of our Kwangtung province have long taken for granted.

By 1832 the British had perfected their steamships; as a result, they met little or no resistance wherever they went. In that year they sent two of their warships to attack Canton. The imperial government ordered Lu Min-su, the governor-general of Liangkwang,[3] to head 3,000 sailors and 20,000 soldiers in defense. Yet Lu, the same man who had once suppressed the Yao[4] rebellion led by the bandit chieftain Chao Chin-lung, was defeated. Having heard about his defeat, Emperor Tao-kuang, in an edict, expressed surprise at Lu's lack of ability in view of his previous success in supressing the Yao rebellion. Lu replied that he was defeated because of the enormous size and power of the enemy's warships, but he could not make himself understood since photography had not yet been invented and the emperor had no comprehension of the capacity of these foreign ships.

It was not until 1840 that Lin Wen-chung[5] first sponsored the translation of foreign newspapers to familiarize the reading public with the situation outside of China. But most Chinese were as ignorant of Western countries as their ancestors had been. During the Opium War, our armed forces were easily defeated at Tinghai and Chushan.[6] This defeat was followed by others; none of our commanders such as Yü-shan, Niu Chien, and Liu Yün-k'o were able to stop the enemy's advance. The enemy's warships entered the Yangtze, and his cannons could be heard as far as Tientsin. Having been defeated, China was forced to open five ports for Western trade. For the first time Emperor Tao-kuang became convinced of the Westerners' strength: the durability of their warships and the efficacy of their cannons. He gave the order that from then on the Chinese should learn to manufacture and use Western weaponry. However, despite his enthusiasm for Western technology, he knew very little about Western countries.

Our defeat during the Opium War was followed by similar defeats in 1849, 1856, 1858, and 1860. We paid an indemnity totaling tens of millions, opened eleven ports for trade, and allowed foreign ministers to reside in Peking. In one instance, foreign troops captured the nation's capital and Emperor Hsien-feng was forced to flee to Jehol. All these were extraordinary occurrences, and our intellectuals should have been awakened by then. But they were not. They continued to look down upon foreigners and shut themselves from foreign contact.

In 1866 Pin-ch'un was ordered to travel around the world, but, being the kind of man he was, he was only interested in amusing himself and did not study foreign countries in a serious or profound manner. Of all the statesmen at that time, only Tseng Wen-cheng,[7] who had done business with Westerners, knew something about Western countries. He established translation bureaus, language schools, and steamship companies. He employed Anson Burlingame, an American, who was accompanied by Chih-kang and Sun Chia-ku, as China's roving ambassador to foreign countries. This was the first time in modern history that a foreigner was employed in this capacity, a situation preceded by the employment of such men as An Shih-na and Chin Jih-shan[8] in ancient times. In any case, this appointment was regarded as unusual and extraordinary by Tseng's contemporaries. Of all of Tseng's recommendations, the most farsighted was perhaps the enrollment in the T'ung-wen Kuan[9] of Hanlin scholars with the fifth rank below who then served in the central government. However, due to the obstruction of such men as Wo Wen-tuan,[10] this recommendation was never carried out. From then on, even though the government had time and again solicited opinions for reforms, our intellectuals continued to resist new ideas because they were so resentful of foreigners.

During the war of 1884, Chang Nan-kuan scored some small success against the French;[11] as a result, he was as much conceited as he was complacent. But, having studied the situation of the world at that time, I was far from being optimistic. Then Russia was coveting the Three Eastern Provinces [Manchuria], and Japan, who had suddenly become strong because of successful reforms, only waited for an opportunity to demonstrate her newly acquired strength by forcibly taking over Korea. Knowing the impending peril, I petitioned our government to adopt reform measures to strengthen ourselves. Many people responded to my recommendation by saying that I was insane.

In 1892 Fu Lan-ya stated in his book *A Brief Account of Translated Books*[12] that the total sale of translated books published by the Shanghai Manufacturing Company amounted to only 10,300 copies. The nation had a population of 400 million; yet only 10,000 people cared to learn about Western affairs through reading translated books, indicating clearly that few of our intellectuals were really interested in knowing anything outside the sphere of China. It took defeat in the war of 1894[13] to wake up our intellectuals once more; after the defeat, one recalls, we had to cede Taiwan to Japan and pay a huge indemnity besides. The pain was great as the wound was deep; it was only then that the more determined intellectuals began to study seriously the causes of our weakness. The mushrooming of patriotic organizations was soon followed by the establishment of a government-operated publishing house and by the publication of numerous newspapers. For the first time in modern history many people began to speak enthusiastically about the "New Learning."

However, no basic reforms were ever carried out after 1894. Here and there some suggestions were made, but these suggestions never went beyond the oratorial stage. Even reforms that were supposedly implemented were only partially effective; this was clearly the case in connection with the building of a strong navy, the construction of telegraphy and railroads, the strengthening of our merchant marine, and shipbuilding. The problem with reform is that one cannot change *A* without in the meantime changing *B* because *A* and *B* are closely related. In other words, the reform on *A* will come to nought if *B* remains unchanged. Even after our defeat in the Sino-Japanese War, we have not purchased one single warship; nor have we doubled our efforts to strengthen our armed forces training program. In 1894, we had 600,000 men in the "green battalions," plus 300,000 under the jurisdiction of the "eight banners." All of these soldiers were either too old or too weak; many of them were actually engaged in their own respective occupations even though their names appeared in the military roster. The Western countries make soldiers out of civilians; we, on the other hand, make civilians out of soldiers. How is it possible for us to fight a successful war against them?

Moreover, the Western countries make a clear distinction between /

the essential and the less significant, and it is to the former that they attach the greatest importance. They stress the importance of schools where students are taught the best ways to preserve and strengthen their own nation. They have parliaments where the voice of the people can be heard; the king is not all-important, nor are the people all-insignificant. Goods produced by the society are not to be one man's monopoly; they are to be enjoyed by all members of the society. In short, the Western practice is in full accord with our Confucian doctrine, and it should not surprise us that these Western countries have become wealthy and strong. We, on the other hand, have consistently neglected our industry, agriculture, and education, as well as our national defense. No workable system has been devised to protect, nourish, and educate the people, and a wide gap exists between the government above and the people below and between the rich and the poor who cannot communicate with each other. Since we have acted in contrary to our own Confucian principles, it is no wonder that we remain as weak as we are.

Our weakness prompted foreign powers to use coercive methods to press their unreasonable demands. In a period of forty days these powers engineered twenty national disasters at our expense. First, Germany demanded the lease of Kiaochow, an event which has become widely known. Second, England wished to impose upon us a loan at an interest of 3 percent, a loan that was viewed with disfavor by the Russians. Third, Germany wanted to open Kiaochow Bay for trade; this, again, was opposed by the Russians. Fourth, France wanted us to open Nanning[14] for trade, and to this the Russians also objected. Fifth, although unable to impose a loan upon us, the British nevertheless succeeded in opening all of our internal rivers to foreign traffic. Sixth, after the Vietnamese had burned some Catholic churches in Saigon, the French forced us to pay an indemnity of 100,000 taels. Seventh, after Yao Hsi-tsan's appointment as governor of Shantung, Germany objected and demanded our government to withdraw the appointment in twenty-four hours; our government, of course, had no choice but to comply with the German demand. Eighth, we proposed to build the Chin-Chen Railroad[15] across the Shantung province, and wired the German government for approval three times. But the German government refused. Ninth, when we redesigned the route so the proposed railroad would pass through Honan instead of Shantung, Germany again raised objections. Approval was finally secured after the British and American ministers had offered their good offices.

Tenth, in the contract whereby Russian advisers were to be employed to train the Nieh Army,[16] it was specifically stipulated that the Russian advisers, instead of the Chinese officers, were the true commanding personnel. Eleventh, these advisers could be retained or dismissed at the pleasure of the Russian czar instead of the Chinese government. Twelfth, Russia succeeded in compelling our government to dismiss four German advisers. Thirteenth, our government was forced to hire Russian advisers in the training of troops in Chihli, Shansi, and the Three Eastern Provinces. Fourteenth, the revenue derived from surtax charges on all commercial traffic along both banks of the Yangtze River was to be assigned to the Shanghai Maritime Customs, a foreign-controlled organization headed by the British interest. Fifteenth, having acquired the territory around Kiaochow, Germany made intensive efforts to acquire more. Sixteenth, having acquired more, she demanded the right to build railroads on it. Seventeenth, having built railroads on it, she complained that the territory was not really large enough and demanded the whole Shantung province as her sphere of influence. Eighteenth, having acquired the whole province, she proceeded to monopolize all industry and commerce in it. Nineteenth, the Russians demanded the cession to them of Dairen, Port Arthur, and Chinchou.[17] Lastly, the French not only demanded the cession of Kwangchow Bay but also insisted that we must not cede Kwangsi, Yunnan, or Kweichow to any other countries.

All the aforesaid events occurred before the second month of this year [1898]. Since then Great Britain has demanded the cession of Weihaiwei, and Japan has imposed upon us another treaty whereby we would not be allowed to cede Fukien to any other power except, of course, Japan.

What has happened to the authority of the Chinese emperor when he has to obtain approval from the German court before he can build a railroad through his own territory and when he in fact cannot even appoint or dismiss his own officials? This is exactly what Chia Yi[18] meant when he said that it was a pity indeed that the emperor of China had become a vassal of the barbarians. In a period of two months, more than twenty national disasters have occurred that involve either loss of territories or encroachment upon our national sovereignty. There are days and years ahead; who knows what the future will bring? If the present situation continues, sooner or later we would have to follow the path of Burma, Annam, India, and Poland and cease to exist as an independent nation. Look at the situation in Poland. When it was partitioned, the foreign powers intimidated its king, insulted its high

exactly

officials, and oppressed and abused its gentry members. Is Poland the road for us to follow? If it is not, what will enable us to escape the fate that has been destined for all weak nations?

After India was conquered by Great Britian, no Indian could become a government official with the sixth rank or above. From 1771 to 1876, in a period of more than 100 years, only two Indians had served as members of parliament. Hong Kong has been British for a long time, and yet no civil service examination has taken place. Shamelessly the Chinese in that colony think of honor or glory in terms of becoming a comprador; meanwhile even the humblest British can look forward to becoming a manager or even a president. There is, say, a Chinese millionaire who formerly occupied the position of a prefectural governor and, for his meritorious service, was once awarded a red or blue button for his hat. Now he is a broker for a foreign firm, standing humbly beside his foreign supervisor whom he must learn to please at all times. What a pity! How pathetic this situation really is! If our country continues to be as weak as she presently is, I am afraid that sometime in the future the best kind of honor we 400 million Chinese can hope for will be no better than that "enjoyed" by this particular Chinese we have described.

During the Yüan Dynasty the Mongols abolished the civil service examination system;[19] under the Mongol rule Chinese intellectuals were treated no better than their modern counterparts in Annam who peddle cloth or silk for a meager livelihood. Thinking about the future, how can we intellectuals not be concerned? Once our country is conquered, are we going to follow the shameless path of serving our new masters, a path that has been viewed with disgust by all the patriots since ancient times? Moreover, once foreigners take over our country, it is unlikely that they could employ us Chinese. To become an official in the Western sense requires specialization in a certain field, since only men with special skills can perform the duties assigned to them. Had Wu Mei-tsun[20] lived under foreign rule, he could not have even found a position as an ordinary teacher; how could he possibly hope to become the head of the Department of Cultural Affairs? Someone might say that if foreigners ever conquer our country, a man like Wu Mei-tsun would follow the example of Hsiung K'ai-yüan by joining the monastic ranks. He does not realize that the Westerners, believing a religion called Christianity, would destroy Buddhism once they take over. After all Buddhist temples in the nation are reduced to ashes, to which temple can a man like Wu Mei-tsun attach himself as a Buddhist monk?

Another man might say that if China is conquered, he could jump into the East China Sea and commit suicide. Since we do not have a navy of our own, the East China Sea is not even ours. The man, in fact, would die in an alien, unpurified place. What can we do? We have 400 million people and tens of thousands of scholars. Is there any road open to us?

Like an army that has recently suffered a decisive defeat, each of us is fighting for his own survival. There is no way to salvation except to exert ourselves and work doubly hard. Hard pressed on a lonely road, we have no choice but to march forward. There cannot be any retreat; nor is there any short cut. Like Han Hsin who was pushed towards the edge of a river and like Hsiang Yü who sank his own ships after passing across the Yangtze,[21] we have no more ground where we can retreat. Only when every Chinese feels this way is there any hope for China's survival.

Yet the government today refuses to speak candidly on the cession of territories and the loss of national sovereignty; it hides them as if they were taboo. Moreover, there are no public media to enable the people to know how dangerous our position really is. In the Paris Museum there are paintings that depict the tragedy of defeat; their purpose is to arouse every Frenchman's patriotism and inspire him to better effort. Our countrymen, not knowing what has happened to their country, remain complacent. They dance and sing as if the world were still an Elysium. They seek fame and fortune in the usual manner, and many of them do not mind violating moral or legal principles as long as they can achieve their goal. Mencius once said: "A country cannot be defeated unless it has already defeated itself." In this sense, we may say that the loss of our territories and the deprivation of our national sovereignty are not a result of foreign coercion or aggression; nor should the whole blame be placed upon our government. We ourselves are the truly guilty ones. If we absolutely refuse to give away our territories, how can we possibly lose any? If we are determined to preserve our national sovereignty, how does any country dare to encroach upon it? In short, if we 400 million Chinese really exert ourselves, how dare any foreigners look down upon us? Yet, instead of exerting ourselves, we are complacent and enjoy ourselves as usual. Who, would you say, are responsible for ceding territories to foreign countries? I, for one, will not blame either our government or the common people. I blame you and me, the intellectuals who have not expressed righteous anger and who in fact have remained undisturbed. If the nation is destroyed, the blame should be squarely placed upon the shoulders of each and everyone of us. If the nation is to be saved, every Chinese has both the right and the obligation to save it.

Once Japan was as weak as China is today. She was pushed around by such countries as England and the United States. Today she is strong enough to conquer Liu-ch'iu, control Korea, and snatch Taiwan from China; she has gone as far as to impose upon us an indemnity payment totaling 200 million taels. Is the strength of the Japanese army responsible for this feat? The answer is no. Should the credit go to the Japanese premier Ito or the Japanese general Oyama? Again the answer is no. It is my considered opinion that the credit for this tremendous achievement should really go to a commoner named Takayama Masa-shiba. Grieved because Japan, a weak nation, could not carry out reforms and resentful of the monopoly of power by the shogunate, he cried for reforms in the streets of Tokyo until he finally died of exhaustion. It was his example that inspired people. . . . The remarkable example of this man shows clearly that an achievement, however great, begins with small simple deeds. How many of us know that the success of modern Japan began with the patriotism of a humble, tactless intellectual named Takayama Masashiba?

Everything's growth requires thermogenetic energy. This energy created heaven as well as the sun. Though the sun is millions of *li* away from the earth, every square foot of the earth receives as much energy as ninety horsepower. Because of the energy it receives, the earth can grow a multitude of things; in fact, wherever there is energy, there is growth. The earth contains magma of extremely high temperature which provides the motive force that makes it rotate all year round without cessation. Before a doctor can forecast a man's life span, he has to first examine the amount of "fire" within the man's body. If the amount of fire has been reduced substantially, the man is going to die. From the above observation we know definitely that heat alone generates growth, luxuriance, expansion, and mobility, while coldness causes shrinkage, weathering, decay, and finally, extinction.

Today we Chinese, by stressing the importance of inactivity, have not completed one worthwhile project. Our soldiers are weak and our scholars are ignorant. We speak approvingly of peace and tranquility and detest any kind of innovations. Meanwhile our territory is snatched away from us piece by piece, and our national sovereignty is rendered less and less effective with the passing of each day. The "fire" within us is flickering out, and we become cold, dry, and decadent. We, in short, are in serious danger.

How can we rescue our nation from its impending extinction? The only way is to increase the thermogenetic energy within ourselves. This energy is essential to those who wish to avenge wrongs and perform great deeds; a man who has lost his will power is a man whose "fire" within himself has been flickering out. Hu Wen-chung[22] once said that China lacked but needed red-blooded, selfless patriots. . . . In ancient literature we often encounter such terms as "martyrs," "men of will," "men of righteousness," and "men of love." One thing that characterizes them is that they are all hot-blooded. The amount of heat one can generate is in direct proportion to size of achievement one can make. It might be as small as that generated by a firefly—if a man cannot generate even that much, he is as good as dead. A great man, on the other hand, generates as much heat as a huge fireball. This heat can make water boil and can scorch anything in sight. Like the heat from the sun, it illuminates as well as burns. The more intensive it is, the more its power of expansion will be. Not only do all things grow under it, but they also grow taller, larger, and more luxuriantly.

In short, there is no way of serving our country except to arouse and enhance our will power. Let not a single moment pass without thinking about our own duties. A prairie fire begins with the striking of a match, and every river originates from a trickle. If we 400 million Chinese bother to arouse ourselves, we can generate enough heat to do whatever we please, and succeed as well. Who, then, can say that our nation cannot be saved?

NOTES

1. This speech was made on April 17, 1898, before an audience gathered at the National Protection Society (Pao-kuo hui) in Peking. Source *Chung-kuo chin-pai-nien Shih-liao*, vol. 1, pp. 501–508.
2. Confucianism.
3. Kwangtung and Kwangsi Provinces.
4. An ethnic minority who lived in Yunnan and Kweichow Provinces.
5. Lin Tse-hsü (1785–1850).
6. Tinghai is a subprefecture located on Chushan Island, off the eastern coast of Chekiang Province.
7. Tseng Kuo-fan (1811–1872).
8. Chin Jih-shan was a Hsiung-nu prince who, after surrendering himself to the Han government, rose to become a cavalry general during the time of Han Wu-ti (r. 140–87 B.C.). An Shih-na cannot be easily identified. The author perhaps had in mind An Lu-shan and Shih Ssu-ming who served the T'ang Dynasty during the eighth century A.D. An was of Tartar origin; Shih, however, was Turkish.
9. A foreign language school in Peking.
10. Wen-tuan was the courtesy name of Wo-jen, an ultraconservative.

11. Nan-kuan was the courtesy name of Chang Shu-sheng, the governor-general of Liangkwang in 1884. In that year one of his generals named Liu Yung-fu defeated the French in Annam.

12. *Yi-shu shih-lioh.*

13. The First Sino-Japanese War (1894–1895).

14. Located in Kwangsi Province.

15. A railroad that linked Tientsin and Chinkiang.

16. An army headed by General Nieh Shih-ch'eng.

17. Located in Liaoning Province, Manchuria.

18. Chia Yi (201–168 B.C.), a famous scholar and essayist of the Han Dynasty.

19. During the Yüan Dynasty the civil service examination was not revived until 1315.

20. Mei-tsun was the courtesy name of Wu Wei-yeh, a famous poet and painter of the seventeenth century.

21. Han Hsin (third century B.C.) was a famous general under Liu Pang, founder of the Han Dynasty. Hsiang Yü (third century *2.3*), a civil war hero, competed with Liu Pang for the vacated Ch'in throne. Later defeated, he committed suicide.

22. Wen-chung was the courtesy name of Hu Lin-yi (nineteenth century), a general and statesman who assisted Tseng Kuo-fan in suppressing the Taiping Rebellion.

LIANG CH'I-CH'AO

The Renovation of the People

After 1900 when the Ch'ing government hesitantly began to follow the Japanese example of modernization, Japan assumed a role of great importance to the Chinese revolution. Large numbers of Chinese students went to Japan to gain "modern" knowledge, and following Japan's victory over Russia in 1905, the figure rose dramatically from 8,000 to 13,000.

Japan at this time was the headquarters not only of the reform leaders who had fled China in 1898, but also of the revolutionaries. In addition to providing an asylum to those who could not disseminate their "dangerous" ideas in China itself, Japan was sympathetic to the revolutionary cause and even helped with funds and weapons.

Among the reform leaders who had found refuge in Japan was Liang Ch'i-ch'ao (1873–1929), a student of K'ang Yu-wei and a brilliant writer. Though he was a "reformer," Liang's articles on such

Reprinted by permission of the publishers from Ssu-yü Teng and John K. Fairbank, *China's Response to the West: A Documentary Survey 1839–1923*, pp. 220–223. Cambridge, Mass.: Harvard University Press, Copyright, 1954, by the President and Fellows of Harvard College.

men as Cromwell, Napoleon, Bismarck, Luther, Voltaire, Rousseau, and Kant provided ideas that went far beyond the framework of the 1898 Reform Movement. Indeed, they became a source of inspiration to many young revolutionaries.

The following article written in 1902 shows how Liang had come to realize that reform in political and economic institutions would not suffice to solve China's problems. The people as a whole needed to be rejuvenated, traditional culture changed, and nationalism promoted.

A state is formed by the assembly of its people. The relationship of a nation to its people resembles that of the body to its four limbs, five viscera, muscles, veins, and corpuscles. There has never been a case where the four limbs have been cut off, the five viscera wasted away, the muscles and veins injured, and the corpuscles dried up, while the body still lived. In the same way, there has never been a nation which could still exist if its people were foolish, timid, disorganized, and confused. Therefore, if we wish the body to live for a long time, the methods of hygiene must be understood. If we wish the nation to be secure, rich, and respectable, the methods for creating a new people must be discussed.

THE RENOVATION OF THE PEOPLE AS THE FIRST AND MOST URGENT MATTER FOR CHINA TODAY

Now I wish to explain thoroughly why a new people is the most urgent and necessary matter. My argument has two bases. One concerns domestic administration and the other concerns diplomatic affairs.

What concerns domestic administration? There are many in the country who are discussing political methods. They would say, A misgoverns the nation or B injures the people; a certain case is a mistake of the government, and a certain system is the fault of officials who have neglected their duty. I do not presume to say that such things are not true. Nevertheless, how is the government formed? Where do the officials come from? Do they not come from among the populace? Is A or B not a member of the citizenry? . . . Why do we have to worry about the lack of a new system, a new government, and a new nation? Even though today we change a law and tomorrow we replace a person, a little painting in the east, a little touch in the west, learning and imitating, I cannot see that there is much help. Why, then, in our country where the new institutions have been discussed for several decades, are the results invisible? It is because we have not yet paid attention to the theory of a new people. . . .

What concerns diplomatic affairs? Since the sixteenth century, about four hundred years ago, the reason for European development and world progress has been the stimulation and growth of extensive nationalist feeling everywhere. What does nationalism mean? It is that in all places people of the same race, the same language, the same religion, and the same customs regard each other as brothers and work for independence and self-government, and organize a more perfect government to work for the public welfare and to oppose the infringement of other races. When this idea had developed to an extreme at the end of the nineteenth century, it went further and became national imperialism within the last twenty or thirty years. What does national imperialism mean? It means that the industrial power of the citizens of a nation has been fully developed domestically and must flow to the outside, and thus they industriously seek to enlarge their powers in other (dependent) regions as appendages. The way of doing it is by military power, commerce, industry or religion, but they use a central policy to direct and protect these activities. . . . Now, on the Asiatic continent there is located the largest country with the most fertile territory, the most corrupt government, and the most disorganized and weak people. As soon as the European race discovered our internal condition, they mobilized their national imperialism as swarms of ants attach themselves to what is rank and foul and as a myriad of arrows concentrate on a target. They were scattered but they concentrated in this corner, the Russians in Manchuria, the Germans in Shantung, the English in the Yangtze valley, the French in Kwangtung and Kwangsi, and the Japanese in Fukien. All are urged on by the tide of the new "ism" (national imperialism). They cannot help doing this. . . .

If we wish to oppose the national imperialism of all the powers today and save China from great calamity and rescue our people, the only thing for us to do is to adopt the policy of promoting our own nationalism. If we wish to promote nationalism in China, there is no other means of doing it except through the renovation of the people.

Today, over the whole country, everybody is worrying about the foreign trouble. Nevertheless, if the foreigners can really cause us trouble, it cannot be ended just by worrying. The stubbornness and aggressiveness of national imperialism is very severe, and yet we are still discussing whether the foreigners can really cause us trouble or not. How foolish we are! I think the existence or non-existence of the trouble will not be decided by the foreigners, but by our domestic condition. In general, all nations are certainly using the same "ism." But why does Russia not apply it to England, and England not apply it to Germany, and Germany not apply it to America, and the various countries of Europe and America not apply it to Japan? It depends on whether there is a chance for doing so or not. . . . Thus, in consideration of present-day China, we must not depend upon a temporary wise emperor or minister to allay the disorder, nor expect a sudden rise of one or two heroes from the rural countryside to lead our struggle for success; it is necessary to have our people's virtue, people's wisdom, and people's power of the whole number of four hundred million all become equal to that of the foreigners—then they naturally cannot cause us trouble and we need not worry about them. . . .

EXPLANATION OF THE MEANING OF "THE NEW PEOPLE"

The term "new people" does not mean that our people must give up entirely what is old in order to follow others. There are two meanings of "new." One is to temper and grind what is original in the people and so renew it; the other is to adopt what was originally lacking in the people and so make a new people. Without one of the two, there will be no success. . . .

Generally, a nation which can endure in the world must have some peculiar characteristics on the part of its nationals. From morals and laws down to customs, habits, literature, and fine arts, all share a kind of independent spirit which has been handed down from grandfather to father and inherited by their descendants. Thus the group is formed and the nation develops. This is really the fundamental source of nationalism. Our people have been established as a nation on the Asiatic continent for several thousand years, and we must have some characteristics which are grand, eminent, and perfect, and distinctly different from those of other races; we should preserve these and not let them be lost. What is called preserving, however, is not to let [the spirit of the people] naturally appear and grow and carelessly say, "I'm preserving it, I'm preserving it." It is like a tree—unless some new boughs come out every year, its withering may soon be expected; as with a well—unless there is always some new spring bubbling, its exhaustion is not far away. Are the new boughs and the new spring coming from the outside? They are old, and yet we cannot but call them new. Only if we can make something new every day can we find the means to keep the old complete. . . .

If we wish to make our nation strong, we must investigate extensively the methods followed by all other nations and races in becoming independent. Selecting their superior points, we can appropriate them to make up our own shortcomings. Now with regard to politics, academic ideas, and techniques, our critics know how to take the superior points of others to fill up our own gaps; but they do not know that the people's virtue, the people's wisdom, and the people's power are really the great source of politics, academic learning, and techniques. If they do not take this but adopt that, neglect the roots but tend the branches, it will be no different from seeing the luxuriant growth of another tree and wishing to graft its branches on to our withered trunk, or seeing the bubbling flow of another well and wishing to take some of the water to fill up our own dry well. Thus, to adopt and make up what we originally lacked in order to renovate our people should be deeply and carefully considered. . . .

All the phenomena in the world are governed by no more than two great principles: one is conservative and the other is aggressive. Those who are applying these two principles are inclined either to the one or to the other. Sometimes the two arise simultaneously and conflict with each other; and sometimes the two exist simultaneously and compromise with each other. No one can exist who is inclined only to one. Where there is conflict, there must be compromise, and conflict is the forerunner of compromise. He who is good at making compromises is a great citizen, such as you find among the Anglo-Saxon race. . . . Thus what I mean by "new people" are not those who are intoxicated with Western customs, despising the morals, academic learning, and customs of our several-thousand-year-old country in order to keep company with others; nor are they those who stick to old paper and say that merely embracing the several thousand years of our own morals, academic learning, and customs will be sufficient to enable us to stand up on the great earth.

TSOU JUNG
Down with the Manchus

Liang Ch'i-ch'ao's prolific writings made thousands of intellectuals become aware of world history and China's crying need for change, but his emphasis on gradual reform to achieve a constitutional monarchy did not gain favor with the radical youth. The extreme nationalism of the revolutionaries came increasingly to be associated with a strong anti-Manchu sentiment. The Manchus were responsible for all the ills in China. The Ch'ing dynasty had to be overthrown and this could only be done by a violent revolution.

The following piece, taken from a tract entitled "The Revolutionary Army," written by an eighteen-year-old student returned from Japan, Tsou Jung, captures the emotionally charged thinking of the revolutionaries and gives an outline of the democratic republic they wished to establish.

The article was published in 1903 in Shanghai, another haven for revolutionaries because of the protection offered by the foreign enclaves. Under pressure from the Ch'ing government Tsou Jung was tried and imprisoned. He died in prison in 1905 and was immediately hailed as a martyr and a revolutionary hero. "The Revolutionary Army" became a best seller and was reprinted several times.

INTRODUCTION

The autocracy of the last few thousand years must be swept away, the slavery of thousands of years abolished. The 5,000,000 barbarian Manchus adorned in their furs, lances, and horns must be destroyed,[1] and the great shame they have inflicted in their 260 years of cruel and harsh treatment expunged, that the Chinese mainland may be purified. All of the Yellow Emperor's[2] descendants can rise to the status of a Washington, rejuvenate themselves, successfully emerge from the 18 stages of hell and ascend to 33 heavenly halls,[3] for their ultimate and resolute aspiration is revolution. Revolution is great!

From a translation of *Ko-ming chün* by Tsou Jung. Shanghai: New China Library, 1912.

I had to skirt the Great Wall for 10,000 *li,* ascend the Kunlun Mountains, swim the Yangtze River, and go upstream on the Yellow River. I raised the flag of independence and struck the bell of freedom, crying out to heaven and earth enough to burst my lungs, to make my voice heard to my fellow countrymen. Alas, for our China today, there must be a revolution!

If our present-day China desires to break the fetters of the Manchus, there must be a revolution! If China wishes to take her place among the great powers, exist in the new world of the twentieth century, attain world-wide recognition, and be respected in her own right in the world, there must be a revolution! Among my fellow countrymen, old, middle-aged, and young, men and women, is there any one who does not speak of revolution? My compatriots burn with fervor to live daily a life of revolution. Now in a loud voice I cry out to proclaim to the world the meaning of revolution.

Revolution! The natural evolution of universal law is revolution. The universal principle of the world is revolution. It is a question of a struggle for survival. This is the essential meaning of this transition period. Revolution is in harmony with the natural order of things and fulfills man's needs.

*   *   *

It grieves me that our fellow countrymen have gone through these numerous barbarian revolutions[4] without achieving an eminent place among the other peoples of the world. I also regret that our countrymen are so readily led by any kind of ruler. Yet, I am glad that my people have now come in contact with enlightened political systems and are able to learn of civilized revolutions. It is fortunate, indeed, that we can now read translations of Rousseau's *Social Contract,* Montesquieu's *Spirit of Laws,* John Stuart Mill's *On Liberty,* French revolutionary history, and the United States "Declaration of Independence." Is that not to my countrymen's advantage?

The profound philosophies of Rousseau and other thinkers are the medicine which can restore the dying soul of China and which the ailing body of the Chinese nation needs to return it to health. These are the fundamental principles upon which French and American civilizations were developed. My country is now sick and dying; is she not in want of good strong tonic to infuse her with new life? If so, I should like to wave the flag of Rousseau and other philosophers over our country.

Besides these philosophies, we have Washington and later Napoleon to set examples of revolution for us. Ah, revolution, revolution! If you have it you will survive, but if you don't you will die. Don't retrogress; don't be neutral; don't hesitate; now is the time! This is why I advocate revolution, so that my fellow countrymen may encourage one another to achieve revolution. If there is anyone who does not want revolution, then he will have to wait hundreds of years until the female Christian messiah who advocated equality and emancipation for the colored people comes to advocate equality and emancipation for the enslaved Chinese.[5]

· · ·

SIGNIFICANCE OF REVOLUTION AND INDEPENDENCE

The British Parliament disobeyed King Charles I because the King extended great privileges to the nobility, endangered the business life of the people, increased taxes arbitrarily, enforced bonds, and collected ship money. The French Revolution was a result of titles given without merit. The difference between the rich and the poor was great. People were not well protected and taxes were levied arbitrarily. These were the reasons for the French patriots' revolt. The Americans struggled for independence because a heavy tea tax and a stamp tax were levied and garrison forces were stationed in America without the consent of the legislature. Consequently, the Americans rose in protest against the British, with the American flag waving at Bunker Hill. I want to reiterate the following over and over again: "The reason for a Chinese revolution in our country today is that as slaves of the Manchus we, the descendants of the Yellow Emperor, have been subject to cruelty and persecution from internal and external sources. We are the slaves of several masters and the slaves of slaves. There is great danger of annihilation of the race."

Since the development of science, the theory of the divinity of the emperor has been toppled. Since the advance of modern civilization, the autocratic system has been overthrown. As people's intelligence and knowledge become more advanced, everyone will be able to enjoy natural rights. The Han people today, in order to throw off the yoke of the Manchus and regain all their lost rights, live among the great powers of the world, and possess the natural rights of freedom and equality, must revolt and then safeguard their independence. I, your humble, uneducated servant, am not qualified to describe the great significance of revolution and independence. With great humility, following the example of the American Revolution, I wish to present to my 400,000,000 Chinese countrymen the following policies for your approval and adoption. Let heaven and earth bear witness:

1. China shall be for the Chinese; our fellow countrymen must realize that China is the China of the Chinese.
2. No alien race shall trespass, not even the slightest, on Chinese rights.
3. All obligations to obey the Manchus shall be abolished.
4. The barbarian Peking government established by the Manchus shall be overthrown.
5. The Manchus living in China shall be expelled or killed in revenge.
6. The Manchu emperor shall be killed in order to do away with the age-old autocratic, monarchial system.
7. All Chinese people and foreign countries hostile to our revolution shall be considered enemies.
8. A central government shall be established as the headquarters of the administration.
9. The country shall be divided into provinces. Each province shall elect one general representative who shall elect a provisional president to represent the nation. One vice president shall be elected as well as representatives from various prefectures and districts.
10. All men and women shall be citizens without regard to sex.
11. All men in the nation shall be obliged to serve in the army.
12. Everyone shall be loyal to the nation.
13. Everyone shall pay taxes.
14. All the people, men and women, shall be equal; there shall be no distinction between the nobility and the commoner.
15. The inalienable rights of the people are given by heaven. The people possess inalienable rights.
16. Life, liberty, and all the other benefits are natural rights.
17. No one shall infringe upon freedom of speech, freedom of thought, or freedom of the press.
18. The people's rights shall be safeguarded, and they should be approved by the public at large. The government shall have the consent of the people and the authority to protect the people's rights.

19. Whenever the government shall interfere with the people's rights, the people shall have the right to revolt against the government in order to secure safety and happiness. Once security and happiness are obtained, then through public discussion the people shall redefine their rights and privileges and establish a new government. This is also the right of the people.

However, after the establishment of the government, if it does not fully meet the expectation of even a minority and the people feel the need to rise up in revolt, then the government will be a very unstable one and this is no way to create a state. Nothing is perfect in the world; the important thing is being peaceful. If the defects of the administration are not really very harmful to the people, then it is better to claim the people's rights by peaceful means than to overthrow the government. However, if the government insists on corrupt ways, then it is not only the right but the obligation of the people to overthrow it and set up a new government to protect their rights. The Chinese people have suffered extreme hardship, and they will not tolerate autocratic government once the independence of revolution is achieved. This is why the political system of the past must be changed.

20. The new nation shall be called "The Republic of China." ("Ch'ing" is the name of a dynasty; "Chih-na" is the name used by the Japanese.)
21. The Republic of China shall be a free and independent nation.
22. This new and independent nation shall have the right to declare war, make peace, and arrange alliances and trade—all the things an independent country is entitled to on an equal footing with the other great powers of the world.
23. Our constitution should be modeled after that of the United States, with the necessary modifications to apply to the situation in China.
24. All self-governing laws shall follow the self-governing laws of the United States.
25. All matters relating to the individual, the whole body of the people, negotiations, the government system, the official system, and all the affairs of the nation shall follow the pattern of the United States.

NOTES

1. During their long rule over China the Manchus had been so sinicized that they could hardly be distinguished from the Han people. By mentioning "furs, lances, and horns" Tsou Jung is trying to exploit the popular image of the Manchus as uncivilized barbarians.

2. I.e., the Han people—descendants of the mythical Yellow Emperor (Huang Ti).

3. This concept is taken from Mahayana Buddhism which has an elaborate description of several heavens and hells.

4. The characters *ko-ming* in the original text should have been translated here as "dynastic changes" and not as "revolution." *Ko-ming,* which has now come to mean revolution, originally meant the withdrawal of the divine mandate from the ruling house, thus leading to its collapse and the establishment of a new dynasty.

5. The reference is unclear.

The Manifesto of the T'ung-meng Hui

Unlike K'ang Yu-wei and Liang Ch'i-ch'ao, Sun Yat-sen (1866–1925) received a nontraditional schooling. He left China when he was thirteen years old and emigrated to Hawaii where he gained Western education and was converted to Christianity. Sun was trained in medicine, but his deep concern for the fate of China led him to become politically active. Unlike K'ang and Liang, he felt that China would be saved by revolution and not reform.

From 1895 on Sun was connected with several unsuccessful uprisings against the Manchu government. By 1905, he came to be regarded as the moving spirit of the revolution. In that year Sun greatly advanced the cause of revolution by bringing together various large and small revolutionary groups and organizations which had so far been acting independently. Although the new organization was still a comparatively small revolutionary party of a few thousand members, the T'ung-meng Hui (The Revolutionary Alliance) platform provided guidelines for future action. The three fundamental principles advanced in the Manifesto of the T'ung-meng Hui—overthrow the Manchus and return China to the Chinese;

Reprinted by permission of the publishers from Ssu-yü Teng and John K. Fairbank, *China's Response to the West: A Documentary Survey 1839–1923*, pp. 227–229. Cambridge, Mass.: Harvard University Press, Copyright, 1954, by the President and Fellows of Harvard College.

establish a republic; and equalize land ownership—were later elaborated into the San Min Chu-i (The Three Principles of the People) by Sun Yat-sen and this became the ideology of the Nationalist Party. Similarly, the three stages by which true constitutional democracy was to be brought to the country later provided legitimacy to certain actions of the Nationalist government.

By order of the Military Government, on the ——— day,———month, ———year of T'ien-yun, the Commander-in-Chief of the Chinese National Army proclaims the purposes and platform of the Military Government to the people of the nation:*

Now the National Army has established the Military Government, which aims to cleanse away two hundred and sixty years of barbarous filth, restore our four-thousand-year-old fatherland, and plan for the welfare of the four hundred million people. Not only is this an unavoidable obligation of the Military Government, but all our fellow-nationals should also take it as their own responsibility. We recall that, since the beginning of our nation the Chinese have always ruled China; although at times alien peoples have usurped the rule, yet our ancestors were able to drive them out and restore Chinese sovereignty so that they could hand down the nation to posterity. Now the men of Han [i.e., the Chinese] have raised a righteous [or patriotic] army to exterminate the northern barbarians. This is a continuation of heroic deeds bequeathed to us by our predecessors, and a great righteous cause lies behind it; there is none among us Chinese who does not understand this. But the revolutions in former generations, such as the Ming Dynasty and the Taiping Heavenly Kingdom, were concerned only with the driving out of barbarians and the restoration of Chinese rule. Aside from these they sought no other change. We today are different from people of former times. Besides the driving out of the barbarian dynasty and the restoration of China, it is necessary also to change the national polity and the people's livelihood. And though there are a myriad ways and means to achieve this goal, the essential spirit that runs through them all is freedom, equality, and fraternity. Therefore in former days there were heroes' revolutions, but today we have a national revolution

---

*The manifesto was also to serve as a proclamation by the local military governments established by successful revolutionary uprisings.

[*Kuo-min ko-ming,* lit., revolution of the people of the country]. "National revolution" means that all people in the nation will have the spirit of freedom, equality, and fraternity; that is, they will all bear the responsibility of revolution. The Military Government is but their agent. From now on the people's responsibility will be the responsibility of the Military Government, and the achievements of the Military Government will be those of the people. With a cooperative mind and concerted effort, the Military Government and the people will thus perform their duty. Therefore we proclaim to the world in utmost sincerity the outline of the present revolution and the fundamental plan for the future administration of the nation.

1. Drive out the Tartars The Manchus of today were originally the eastern barbarians beyond the Great Wall. They frequently caused border troubles during the Ming Dynasty; then when China was in a disturbed state they came inside Shanhaikuan, conquered China, and enslaved our Chinese people. Those who opposed them were killed by the hundreds of thousands, and our Chinese have been a people without a nation for two hundred and sixty years. The extreme cruelties and tyrannies of the Manchu government have now reached their limit. With the righteous army poised against them, we will overthrow that government, and restore our sovereign rights. Those Manchu and Chinese military men who have a change of heart and come over to us will be granted amnesty, while those who dare to resist will be slaughtered without mercy. Chinese who act as Chinese traitors in the cause of the Manchus will be treated in the same way.

2. Restore China China is the China of the Chinese. The government of China should be in the hands of the Chinese. After driving out the Tartars we must restore our national state. Those who dare to act like Shih Ching-t'ang or Wu San-kuei [both were traitors] will be attacked by the whole country.

3. Establish the Republic Now our revolution is based on equality, in order to establish a republican government. All our people are equal and all enjoy political rights. The president will be publicly chosen by the people of the country. The parliament will be made up of members publicly chosen by the people of the country. A constitution of the Chinese Republic will be enacted, and every person must abide by it.

Whoever dares to make himself a monarch shall be attacked by the whole country.

4. *Equalize land ownership* The good fortune of civilization is to be shared equally by all the people of the nation. We should improve our social and economic organization, and assess the value of all the land in the country. Its present price shall be received by the owner, but all increases in value resulting from reform and social improvements after the revolution shall belong to the state, to be shared by all the people, in order to create a socialist state, where each family within the empire can be well supported, each person satisfied, and no one fail to secure employment. Those who dare to control the livelihood of the people through monopoly shall be ostracized.

The above four points will be carried out in three steps in due order. The first period is government by military law. When the righteous army has arisen, various places will join the cause. The common people of each locality will escape from the Manchu fetters. Those who come upon the enemy must unite in hatred of him, must join harmoniously with the compatriots within their ranks and suppress the enemy bandits. Both the armies and the people will be under the rule of military law. The armies will do their best in defeating the enemy on behalf of the people, and the people will supply the needs of the armies, and not do harm to their security. The local administration, in areas where the enemy has been either already defeated or not yet defeated, will be controlled in general by the Military Government, so that step by step the accumulated evils can be swept away. Evils like the oppression of the government, the greed and graft of officials, the squeeze of government clerks and runners, the cruelty of tortures and penalties, the tyranny of tax collections, the humiliation of the queue—shall all be exterminated together with the Manchu rule. Evils in social customs, such as the keeping of slaves, the cruelty of foot-binding, the spread of the poison of opium, the obstructions of geomancy *(feng-shui)*, should also all be prohibited. The time limit for each district (*hsien*) is three years. In those *hsien* where real results are achieved before the end of three years, the military law shall be lifted and a provisional constitution shall be enacted.

The second period is that of government by a provisional constitution. When military law is lifted in each *hsien*, the Military Government shall return the right of self-government to the local people. The members of local councils and local officials shall all be elected by the people. All rights and duties of the Military Government toward the people and those of the people toward the government shall be regulated by the provisional constitution, which shall be observed by the Military Government, the local councils, and the people. Those who violate the law shall be held responsible. Six years after the securing of peace in the nation the provisional constitution shall be annulled and the constitution shall be promulgated.

The third period will be government under the constitution. Six years after the provisional constitution has been enforced a constitution shall be made. The military and administrative powers of the Military Government shall be annulled; the people shall elect the president, and elect the members of parliament to organize the parliament. The administrative matters of the nation shall proceed according to the provisions of the constitution.

Of these three periods the first is the period in which the Military Government leads the people in eradicating all traditional evils and abuses; the second is the period in which the Military Government gives the power of local self-government to the people while retaining general control over the national affairs; the third is the period in which the Military Government is divested of its powers, and the government will by itself manage the national affairs under the constitution. It is hoped that our people will proceed in due order and cultivate their free and equal status; the foundation of the Chinese Republic will be entirely based on this.

[The last paragraph of the manifesto consists of an exhortation to the Chinese people to rise to the occasion, support the ever-faithful Military Government, and shoulder the responsibility of protecting the country and preserving their own ancient and superior race.]

MARY CLABAUGH WRIGHT*
A New Society in the Making

In an earlier reading we saw how K'ang Yu-wei had strongly recommended that China try to follow the Japanese model. After the Boxer debacle in 1900 the Imperial government of China at last began to take measures to modernize some government institutions and it did indeed look to Japan for inspiration. Japan was the first Asian state to prove that a non-European nation could successfully borrow from the West, and in so doing acquire the strength to resist the West.

The bloodless revolution achieved in Japan under the guise of "restoring" power to the Emperor could not, however, be duplicated in China. Every step toward modernization taken by the Ch'ing government only helped to undermine the support offered by tradition to the Imperial institution. The government, in fact, in many ways helped prepare the ground for revolution and its own demise.

The following excerpt describes the nature of the changes that took place in Chinese society between 1900 and 1911.

China after 1900 was in many ways a new world, the result in part of the same forces that led to the imperial reforms and in part of the changes introduced by those reforms. From the heart of China, G. E. Morrison reported: "No one who has seen the change which is taking place in the country served by the [Peking-Hankow] railroad can long remain pessimistic as to the future of China."[1] And he found similar changes in Sinkiang in the far northwest: population and revenues were increasing, a modernizing spirit was felt everywhere, the vigorous campaign against opium was making progress, able officials were on the job, and corruption was less easy.[2]

Rapidly improving communications made it possible for groups in widely separated parts of the country to act simultaneously, as the

From Mary Clabaugh Wright, ed., *China in Revolution: The First Phase 1900–1913* (New Haven: Yale University Press). Copyright © 1968 by Yale University (second printing 1971), pp. 30–44. Reprinted by permission.

*Mary C. Wright was Professor of History at Yale University till her untimely death a few years ago. She is also author of *The Last Stand of Chinese Conservatism: The T'ung-chih Restoration 1862-1874,* Stanford: Stanford University Press, 1957, third printing 1967.

boycotts and other popular protests showed. Railways and telegraph lines were rapidly being extended. The postal service expanded along with and beyond the lines of the railways.

. . . A veteran China journalist of ten years' experience concluded:

> For the first time in history the Chinese have discovered a common ground of union which has appealed to men of all classes and trades, of all religions, and all sections of the community. Unconsciously the Chinese have welded themselves into a nation.[3]

There was a different look to the cities. From Peking to Chengtu, streets were being cleaned, paved, and lighted. They were well policed and crime seemed no threat. New buildings were under construction. Beggars and prostitutes were becoming a rare sight except in the foreign-dominated ports. It was reported that they had been rounded up for vocational training in special institutes,[4] not by order of the central government but through the cooperation of municipal officials and the various new citizens' organizations, in a burst of civic pride. Customs too were changing. Everywhere there were local societies to stamp out footbinding, gambling, opium smoking—anything that was regarded as one of the evils of Old China.

Newspapers were a prime force in expressing and in turn reinforcing this emergent public opinion. Their numbers and their distribution expanded rapidly. Travelers found an ample supply of newspapers at all the stopping places of the riverboat service on the Yangtze and reported that Chinese provincial readers were better informed about world affairs than the readers of the European provincial press. Others reported that while in 1895 the people only knew that China had been beaten, by 1908 any schoolboy could give a fairly accurate account of the Russo-Japanese War. The press was sufficiently informative for a village teacher who had never left home to discuss, with an interested local audience, the coming constitution, educational policy, and changes in the appointments of high officials.

The press affected politics directly as well as indirectly. In one case, for example, the governor-general at Nanking wrote letters to the papers explaining policies for which he had been attacked. The press also provided an alternative hearing for the victim of an alleged miscarriage of justice. Formerly he could petition the governor, of course, but he had no way of commanding the governor's attention. Now he could write a letter to a newspaper which the governor would read and, in most cases, investigate.

The magazines of the time, even those that were purely commercial ventures, concentrated on educating the literate public to China's needs; the contents of these magazines, like those of the newspapers, were then spread by word of mouth beyond their immediate office. In literature the realistic novel, often serialized, was predominant. Bitterness over the Allied occupation of Peking in 1900, nationalism, and satires on officials were recurrent themes. Even the archconservative Lin Shu elected to translate *Uncle Tom's Cabin*. The theater followed fiction's example: the old heroic legends and bawdy comedies were giving way to a patriotic repertory. Apparently this was what the audiences wanted, since the playwright-director had to count on paid admissions to cover expenses.

In this new world, old classes were changing and new classes emerging. *But several of those most important to the developing revolutionary movement were dynamic new groups that it would be difficult to call social classes.** Therefore I shall not base this brief discussion on an account of how the old four-class (scholar [gentry], peasant, artisan, merchant) society had broken down, but rather begin with the new groups and classes that were being formed and proceed to the old classes that were being transformed.

YOUTH

Students, and youth generally, were in many ways the most important group to gain prominence in China in the first phase of the revolution. There had been many upheavals in China's long history, but only after 1900 did young people, mainly from the new schools, take the lead. It is a Western truism that the younger generation is seldom satisfied with the world left them by their elders. This has obscured the significance of the fact that in a country where, more than anywhere else, youth had bowed to the authority of age both in times of peace and in times of crisis, youth—precisely because of its lack of trammeling experience and of habitual acceptance of the world as it is—suddenly became the most vibrant force in the nation. The Chinese youth movement, of which we have not yet seen the end, began in this period rather than in 1919. The May Fourth Movement was its second stage, not its origin.

Intelligence, courage, and indifference to death for their cause gave the new youth an influence out of all proportion to their numbers. One

*Italics added.

of them, as a schoolteacher, could start the awakening of a whole county. One of them, in a military training school or army unit, could give shape to the passionate but often formless ideas that were abroad everywhere. At the same time, the social position they had inherited and the respect with which they were listened to in a country accustomed to respecting the educated gave them something of the aura of the old elite even as they called for its destruction.

As is well known, the most politically active youth studied in Japan, where many of the reformist and revolutionary organizations and journals were based. In addition, some who were from southwest China picked up their new ideas in British Burma or French Indochina, where the contrast between the English and French books they read and the behavior of British and French colonials toward natives seemed to them to underscore the significance of Western European liberal and radical ideas. Those who studied in America or Europe were on the whole younger, and they were widely scattered in countries where Chinese politics were of little interest. They tended to study technical subjects and on the whole had little interest in or influence on the revolutionary movement at this time.*

• • •

WOMEN

Girls and young women played a prominent role in the revolutionary youth movement. Many of the activists attended the new girls' schools established by the imperial reforms or the private schools that wealthy high officials had done so much to encourage. In Canton, where girls of good family had lived entirely within the family courtyard until a few years before, girl students joined the patriotic demonstrations over the *Tatsu Maru* case in 1908. Thousands were reported to have marched out of their academies to hold meetings, wearing mourning white and rings engraved "National Humiliation." On April 6 they joined other women of Canton in forming a National Humiliation Society. Their fainting at emotionally supercharged meetings was interpreted as showing the depths of their despair for the country, as the first step toward suicide, the final protest. There is no doubt that such news, dramatized in the press but based on fact, contributed to the revolutionary élan of the era.

*It must be remembered that the number of students who went to Japan far exceeded those in other countries. (Editor)

In even more conservative Foochow, girls formed a Patriotic Society to which they contributed their jewelry, and when the revolution broke out, they, like the girl students of Canton, struggled for the right to fight. At their meetings they were described as looking tiny and dainty, weary, but determined. In Shanghai, where old customs yielded sooner, there was in 1910 a wave of militant, defiant, nationalist demonstrations by well-disciplined schoolgirls and their teachers.

China's new feminism took many forms. When the revolution broke out in Wuchang, it was the boatwomen of the Canton area who went to the revolutionary front, probably the first nurses ever assigned to Chinese troops in combat. At the other extreme, one of the new journals said to be read by court ladies, *Pei-ching nü pao* (Peking Woman), ran a series of articles on the equality of all human beings. In some areas, women won the right to participate in the new provincial organs of self-government. The militant woman schoolteacher quickly emerged as a new "type." . . . Sophia Chang, who adopted the personal name of the Russian revolutionary heroine Sophia Perovskaya, was a leader in the Revolutionary Alliance. She organized the women of Shanghai and raised funds through performances of plays dealing with three great revolutions: the American,[5] the French, and, as the final culmination, the Chinese. She too was a schoolmistress, and there were many like her throughout the country.

The new sense of freedom reached beyond politics. Women were increasingly seen in public, and footbinding was starting to die out. . . . The shift in the position and aspirations of women was as swift and dramatic as the shift in the role of youth as a whole. Chinese women had traditionally been less confined than women in many countries—they had ranged all the way from the dominating wives of henpecked peasant husbands to the talented daughters privately tutored on the insistence of doting fathers. But they had been subject not only to legal disabilities but to social pressures and a code of behavior that kept them—whether sheltered or shackled—at home.

The change in the position of women, like that of youth, was lasting and irreversible, as the later history of China has shown. In this sense, it was one of the hallmarks of a major social revolution.

THE NEW MILITARY MEN

The military had played a prominent role in most periods of Chinese history, and the predominant role more than once, but the officers and men of the new armies constituted a genuinely new group. The imperial government wanted officers and soldiers of a new stamp, and they succeeded in getting more than they had perhaps intended. According to the well-informed correspondent of the London *Times,* "The Chinese soldier of today is a different man from his fellow of even ten years ago."[6] . . .

An Anglo-Indian journalist concluded after a tour of training facilities and arsenals that they "are turning out officers as different from the past as the modern Mauser rifles and cartridges which the factories are producing by the hundred thousand and the million, are different from the ancient blunderbusses with which the Chinese of yesterday were armed."[7]

The professional accomplishments of the military reform program are well attested, as I have indicated above in discussing the imperial reforms. Morale was good because of vastly improved organization and because the men believed that they could become heroes in the national drive to repel the foreigner and to restore China to greatness.

Once the revolution broke out, however, there are scores of witnesses to the vastly superior morale both of the imperial units who went over to the republican side and of the raw, hastily recruited new revolutionary units. There were loyal imperial forces who did not collapse but they seemed to have lost their former sense of purpose and to be fighting from habit rather than from conviction; they certainly lacked the passionate élan of their revolutionary adversaries.

• • •

There is considerable evidence to suggest that the new armies—first the imperial forces and later the revolutionary forces were more than agents of modernization in the upper strata of Chinese society. They may have been the agency through which part of the peasantry too was involved in the Chinese Revolution from the outset. . . .

THE OVERSEAS CHINESE

The first phase of the Chinese Revolution marked the emergence into the national public life of a fourth new group—the Overseas Chinese. For generations, despite legal prohibitions, Chinese, especially from the overcrowded southeastern provinces, had been emigrating to Southeast Asia and more recently to the Americas and Africa. A few became wealthy, and a large number became reasonably prosperous by moving in to supply whatever skills or services were lacking and in demand.

The majority were shipped out in the notorious coolie trade to meet the demand for labor in Africa, Borneo, or building American railways. Those who lived made their way up. But assimilation to the areas in which they settled did not begin until much later. All their loyalties were focused on their native places in China, but the most they could hope for was to send money home and eventually to be buried there.

With the turn of the century, all factions of New China sought their support. The imperial government made more vigorous efforts to control the coolie trade and to establish Chinese consulates to look after the welfare of its overseas subjects. Many returned home and found careers in the new enterprises. The reformers and the revolutionaries who traveled abroad contended for the support of the Chinese communities wherever they went. Sun Yat-sen's Society to Restore China's Prosperity and several ephemeral early revolutionary groups were essentially Overseas Chinese organizations.

Not all Overseas Chinese were revolutionaries; the reformers had their following and the Overseas communities would have sent their representatives to the Imperial Parliament scheduled to convene in 1913. But in a broader sense, all the Overseas Chinese—offered a place in Chinese public life for the first time, adding a new and different element to the new public opinion—were, like the new youth, the new woman, and the new military, a revolutionary social force.

•   •   •

THE WORKING CLASS

The fifth of the new groups to enter Chinese public life and politics was the small working class. Here I mean not the traditional artisans, although apparently they often took part in nationalist demonstrations, but the workers employed in such modern industries as textiles, railways, and mining. Despite their small numbers, there were large concentrations of them at critical times and places. In October of 1911, for example, there were 6,000 railway workers fron North China in the Yangtze River port of Ichang.[8]

. . . The workers shared the general anti-imperialist mood of the times and, for example, refused to unload Japanese ships following the *Tatsu Maru* incident. The number of strikes rose sharply whenever political tension was heightened; the period just prior to the outbreak of the Revolution of 1911 was one of the peaks.[9]

These new industrial workers were recruited not from the artisanate but directly from the poorer peasantry, and they maintained close ties with their villages. They were important in this period because they could put teeth into protests initiated by others and because, with their periodic visits home, they constituted one of the channels through which the new ideas were beginning to affect the so-called vast immovable mass of the Chinese peasantry.

The five new groups on the political scene—youth, women, the modern military, the Overseas Chinese, and industrial labor—make a strange company, but they have in common several important features. All had been subject to more than average deprivation in traditional Chinese society; all were in situations where they were more aware than most of what foreign pressure had cost China; all were in positions where action seemed possible; all had a less than average stake in the preservation of existing institutions. This of course does not mean that they constituted a solid revolutionary phalanx. Obviously as the first phase of the revolution subsided many students decided to get on with their careers, many women to look after their households, many Overseas Chinese to make fortunes, and many workers to save a little money to buy land to reenter the landowning peasantry. What it does mean is that there were substantial groups, volatile because of their newness, with sharp discontents, each capable of a distinct and major contribution to the creation of a New China. The educated and aroused young could analyze China's plight and fire off ideas—some sparks, some rockets. The soldiers could offer their training and their arms. The Overseas Chinese—the poor as well as the rich—could provide money and entrepreneurial and technical skills. The workers could back up their ideas with strikes that really hurt.

This was an impressive revolutionary striking force—many revolutions have succeeded with less—but none of its components was central to existing Chinese society. The Chinese "establishment" was vast and deeply rooted. I therefore turn now to change, and resistance to change, among existing classes: the gentry, merchants, and peasants.

THE GENTRY

For centuries the Chinese gentry had gained access to public office through the Examination System. Their status carried with it a host of tangible and intangible benefits: a virtual monopoly of the higher culture, leisure, great respect and deference, certain legal immunities, and opportunities to accumulate land. They were the social class with the highest stake in the old order. The question here is whether this class was undergoing significant change after 1900, and if so in what ways.

There are enough studies to show that the gentry of the nineteenth century and earlier were very different from what was called the gentry in community studies of the 1930s and 1940s. The slim evidence that we have suggests that this transformation of the gentry began and progressed surprisingly far in the decade after 1900. The abolition of the Examination System in 1905 destroyed the primary basis of their status. They were quick to see this and to adjust to it by preparing their children for the newly opening careers in business and the professions, and for posts in a quite different kind of government. Land rents were important—they remained so until 1949—but it was a rare gentry family that could live on land rents alone; holdings even of substantial gentry families were quickly broken up through the equal division of property among all sons and the provision of substantial dowries for daughters. This process was not new; what was new was the availability of new occupations and sources of income.

There can have been scarcely a gentry family that did not include a radical student, and officer in the new armies, or an investor in modern enterprises. The gentry do not seem to have been isolated from the main currents of the time. They read newspapers and wrote letters to the editor. They were the leaders of the local self-government associations and dominated the provincial assemblies. . . . The records show that these organizations concentrated on the great national issues of the day: resistance to Western encroachment, domestic social reforms, constitutional government.

•　•　•

I have no doubt that many gentry families compromised on all sides to stay out of trouble. Men like Chang Ping-lin, at this time a far more radical revolutionary than Sun Yat-sen, were members of the gentry and maintained their gentry connections. New entrepreneurs like Chang Chien, a member of the exalted upper reaches of the gentry, were leaders in the assemblies and in the constitutional movement.

•　•　•

THE BOURGEOISIE

Merchants in imperial China had suffered from both legal disabilities and lack of social standing. Some had been enormously wealthy, but their position was always precarious. Confiscatory taxes in the form of forced contributions to the state were not uncommon, and merchant property was always in jeopardy. In these circumstances, merchants had to curry favor with officials, and they nearly always attempted to escape upward into the scholar-gentry class by educating their sons for the official examinations. All these factors prevented the emergence of a strong, self-conscious, independent merchant class.

The opening of the treaty ports provided new opportunities for merchants, and their numbers greatly expanded. By the beginning of the twentieth century it was beginning to be recognized that they had an essential role to play in the development of the Chinese economy by Chinese rather than foreigners. As the foundations of gentry status were undermined, many members of the gentry saw the advantages of modern enterprise. A new class, a bourgeoisie, was thus recruited from both the merchants and the gentry of traditional society. Merchants took their place, long denied, in the councils of the local elite and a new compound term, gentry-merchant (*shen-shang*), came into general use. . . .

Some merchants in the older handicraft centers remained aloof from the new currents and continued to work, and sometimes to live, with their artisans in the old way and in relatively small units. So did merchants at the street stall or peddler level. All these seem to have taken part in the nationalist demonstrations, but apparently they were not part of the flow either into the nascent bourgeoisie or into the nascent industrial labor force. The continued existence of these master-apprentice units, located in areas where wealthy Chinese and foreigners were concentrated and producing articles for their use, perhaps contributed to the persistent myth of an unchanging China.

•   •   •

Nonetheless, when it came the revolution was distinctly not a bourgeois revolution; the bourgeoisie's role was important but always auxiliary. They were, along with the gentry, leaders in the constitutional movement and in the formation of a new public opinion. When fighting broke out, they sometimes gave the revolutionaries active support without thought of property loss—local variations were enormous on this point—but generally they attempted to work out an orderly transfer to power; for long periods their chambers of commerce were often the only stable source of authority.

There is a strange discrepancy between the interests and role of the bourgeoisie and its ideology. Its members talked vaguely but passionately of liberty, equality, and fraternity; of nationalism, democracy, and mass welfare. These ideas were neither coherently thought out nor expressive of their class interests, for theirs was in no way the position of the French bourgeoisie in the eighteenth century. Yet the very fact that these words, however poorly understood, were so constantly used, may have been one of the most important contributions of the bourgeoisie to the revolutionary movement.

•   •   •

THE PEASANTRY

To what degree did the revolutionary changes of the early twentieth century affect the peasantry? Were the peasants, as some have claimed, largely ignorant of what was going on in the upper layers of society, a passive mass that was indifferent unless one or another of the contesting parties pressed them too hard in the demand for grain and manpower? Or were they ready to provide a mass base for revolution if the revolutionary leaders had only understood how to reach them?

Here I think we must recognize the illogical but real distinction between the "people of China" and the peasantry who constituted 80 percent of that people. It is clear that the British minister was greatly in error when he reported that the revolution was based on "the usual platitudes about the struggle for freedom . . . in which not more than five percent of the population of China take the slightest interest." The Foreign Office found this "remarkable" in view of the information coming in, but noted that even so, 5 percent of the population of China was 20,000,000 people.[10]

It is abundantly clear that considerably more than 5 percent of the population was involved in the massive boycotts and demonstrations. . . . The people of China were certainly affected by and contributing to these changes, if by people one means the visible 20 percent. One need only recall . . . that the proportion of the electorate expanded from 1 percent of the adult male population in 1909 to 25 percent in 1912; or that the signatures to the petitions demanding a speedier convening of a parliament expanded from a reported 200,000 signatures in June 1910 to a reported 25 million in October of that year. In my opinion, on the evidence now available, these changes were also reaching into the peasantry.

The fallacy of an inert peasantry that characterized so many contemporary accounts and continues, in my view, to distort research, was well expressed by a careful observer who was, surprisingly, General Frey of the French colonial army. In his opinion, there was ample evidence of the nationalism of the Chinese peasant: that he was concerned with the fate of the country as a whole at the hands of foreigners and with the problems of remote areas within China. Frey attributed widespread European belief in the self-centeredness of a self-sufficient peasantry to the fact that many of the writers had little knowledge of the Chinese countryside and were prone to generalize on the basis of their acquaintance with what he called the mercenary uprooted Chinese of the coastal cities. He pointed out that peasants must work without interruption or starve.[11] The fact that they continued to work in the fields did not prove that their interests were limited to those fields. General Frey presumably reached this conclusion from close observation of Chinese soldiers, who were of course peasants.

A veteran English journalist reported that the societies protesting the American Exclusion Act of 1905 served as links through which reform groups "now reach and direct social forces which have hitherto lain beyond their control."[12] One should remember that the people being excluded from the United States were mainly peasants, certainly the poor. Another long-time resident and close observer summarizing the various changes—the press, foreign trade, new schools, the postal service, the activities of the provincial assemblies—concluded: " . . . all had combined, without perhaps changing the people, gradually to accustom them to the idea of change. It is a process that has gone deeper and had more considerable consequences than is generally supposed."[13]

Since the issue is still speculative, let us turn the question around. The new armies were recruiting and indoctrinating peasant troops who displayed high morale. The industrial labor force, removed from the peasantry only seasonally, was calling patriotic strikes. Newspapers were widely disseminated and they emphasized national and international issues; these were read aloud in villages by old literati trying to catch up with the times as well as by students from the new schools. Storytellers and traveling theater troupes played up the themes of New China to peasant audiences. How reasonable is it to suppose that Chinese peasants, illiterate but cultivated and excellent conversationalists, let all this pass them by, and talked only of crops and marriages in the hours of teahouse talk on market days?

One qualified observer found them poorly informed on politics, but highly responsive to revolutionary slogans:

They possess the moral qualities that go to the making of a great nation. . . . They could be a great power in the hands of anyone who could coordinate their scattered units and induce them to follow his lead.[14]

NOTES

1. From Sianfu, Jan. 31, 1910, in the *Times* (London, March 3,1910).
2. From Urumchi, May 5, 1910, in the *Times* (London, June 13, 1910).
3. Douglas Story, *Tomorrow in the East* (London, 1907), pp. 170-73.
4. Roger Sprague, *From Western China to the Golden Gate* (Berkeley, 1911), pp. 107–13. The author had taught English in the new Chinese schools and knew the Chinese language.
5. The magnitude and radicalism of the American Revolution were curiously overestimated in China at this time. Washington was the one Western name known everywhere. I have found one case where it was taken to mean the president of any republic.
6. G. E. Morrison, quoted in F. A. McKenzie, "Four Hundred Million Chinamen Awaken" (an interview with Morrison), *The London Magazine*, 25, no. 150 (February 1911), pp. 702–03.
7. Everard Cotes, *Signs and Portents in the Far East* (London, 1907), pp. 22–23.
8. FO 371/1089, no. 52197.
9. Jean Chesneaux, *The Chinese Labor Movement, 1919–1927* (Stanford, Calif., 1968). (Original French edition 1962.)
10. FO 371/15, no. 952. The Foreign Office cover minute was marked for the attention of the cabinet.
11. General H. Frey, *L'Armée chinoise* (Paris, 1904), pp. 85–95.
12. Story, *Tomorrow in the East*, p.173.
13. Percy H. Kent, The Passing of the Manchus (London, 1912), pp. 63–64. The author was legal adviser to the (Chinese) supervisor of industries in Chihli Province.
14. Fernand Farjenel, *Through the Chinese Revolution*, trans. Margaret Vivian (London, 1915), p. 142. The author, who taught courses on China at the Collège Libre des Sciences Sociales, traveled in China immediately before and during the revolution.

II The Cultural Revolution and Nationalism

The revolutionaries played an important role in spreading disaffection among the various sections of Chinese society, but they were not well organized and lacked a clearly articulated ideology. They also lacked funds, were militarily weak, and had little mass support. The 1911 Revolution was, therefore, only partially successful. It ended the two-thousand-year-old Confucian state but the revolutionaries had to compromise and accept General Yüan Shih-k'ai, head of the Imperial forces, as the President of the Republic of China. Their hope that President Yüan could be controlled by a constitutional system of government was soon destroyed when Yüan assumed dictatorial power. In 1915 he even tried to set himself up as emperor.

A newly established government, even in the traditional style, would have faced innumerable problems. To replace the Confucian imperial system with a constitutional republic was a dream impossible to realize. Western institutions like the parliament and the cabinet could not be grafted onto the existing Chinese body politic.

Chinese intellectuals, disillusioned and frustrated, began to re-examine the problem of modernization, and came to the conclusion that tradition had to be abandoned *in toto* and a "new culture" created so that the nation could be remade. The fact that a conservative movement to revive Confucianism had been closely linked with attempts to restore monarchy confirmed the suspicion that Confucian ethics and institutions could still be used to suppress the people and thwart the revolution.

From 1911 to 1927 the government of China can be ignored as a source of change. Indeed the warlord decade (1916–1927) was a period of political chaos, but if we turn our attention to social and intellectual developments we notice happenings of great promise.

The revolution moved temporarily into nonpolitical channels only to strengthen the spirit of nationalism and thereafter return to its political course, revitalized and more broadly based.

WOLFGANG FRANKE*
1911 and the New Republic

The following selection highlights the significance of the 1911 Revolution. It also indicates the problems which the young republic faced and the reasons for the failure of the Republican revolution.

The revolution of 1911 and the consequent establishment of a republic had a quite extraordinary significance, far exceeding that of the abolition of monarchies in European countries such as France in 1870 or Germany in 1918. In China the year 1911 put an end to a development stretching over 2,000 years or even longer without any serious break. The Confucian view of the state, continuing earlier traditions, had held sway in China without serious opposition since the beginning of the Christian era. In the course of the centuries this universalistic view of the state and the world had been modified and developed in detail, without any of its essential foundations, such as the position and authority of the Emperor as Son of Heaven, being seriously affected. Even the foreign dynasties—Tungus, Mongols and Manchus, etc.—which ruled China temporarily, for the most part adopted the Chinese view of the state. Only in the 19th century, as a result of changed conditions, did it become clear that this traditional view was untenable and that the Confucian idea of the state was simply Utopian. Hence the revolution of 1911 meant the final overthrow of a structure that had been shaken by Western imperialism from without and slowly but surely undermined and ruined from within ever since the Taiping revolution, not least by the abolition of the official examination system. It is important to notice that the revolution of 1911 was not just another of the many changes of dynasty which China had often experienced, even though it had many of the characteristic elements of such changes and was soon followed by an attempt to establish a new dynasty. Nor

Reprinted from pp. 75–84 of *A Century of Chinese Revolution, 1851–1949*, by Wolfgang Franke, by permission of the University of South Carolina Press. Copyright © 1970 by the University of South Carolina Press.

*Wolfgang Franke was at the Sino-German Cultural Institute in Peking from 1937 to 1945, professor at two Chinese universities at Chengtu 1946–1948, and at Peking University 1948–1950. Later he became professor and director of the Institute of Chinese Language and Culture at the University of Hamburg.

was it, as it may perhaps have seemed at the beginning, the introduction of a new era of division and strife, with each ruler declaring himself the legitimate successor of the Son of Heaven. It was much more the conclusion of an era, an era of more than 2,000 years, the irrevocable end of the Confucian state and indeed of Confucianism. Since the beginning of this century and particularly since 1911 China has found itself in a tremendous crisis, the dimensions and significance of which have rarely been seen in the history of the world; the number of those involved in this crisis is about equal to the entire population of Europe. All traditional political, social, intellectual and moral foundations, which had for centuries been regarded as inviolable dogma, indubitably true and self-evident, were reduced to absolutely nothing, to a mere shadow. China has been compared to an old man, who has spent his whole life in the service of a certain idea, believing in its truth and making important contributions based on this idea, and who has suddenly realized in extreme old age that all his presuppositions and ideas have been false and untenable.

These far-reaching consequences of the revolution may have been clear to only a few—inside and outside China. Sun Yat-sen and his followers were full of idealistic and unselfish aims and they deserve credit for having administered the final blow to the tottering Confucian state. In a sense, therefore, their work was essentially destructive. They were not in a position, however, to do anything conclusive or radically new to replace the old order they had destroyed. Their ideas about building up the republic, such as the Three People's Principles and the Five Power Constitution, were too theoretical and took no account of the existing situation. The theoreticians of the revolution lacked insight into the political possibilities afforded by the historical conditions. They lived in a world of theory rather than reality. It was no new experience in Chinese history to have elaborate theoretical systems drawn up and discussed without reference to their practicability; and it would be unfair to expect the revolutionaries to have erected even the foundations of a new structure, while the old decaying structure was still collapsing. The politically inexperienced, idealistic revolutionary theoreticians were confronted by the politically cunning and unscrupulous 'war-lords' and their followers. By far the most capable among them was Yüan Shih-k'ai. He possessed political experience and subtlety, knew what had happened in the past, and could make an accurate assessment of the present situation while exploiting the personal opportunities open to him. He had at his disposal everything that the revolutionaries needed, but he lacked their idealism and sense of responsibility. His activities served no higher purpose or aim than his own ambition and desire for power.

The collapse of the dynasty and the traditional view of the state meant the end of the only bond that had held China together throughout long centuries of real political division. The centrifugal regional forces in the different parts of the country which had slumbered for several centuries, began to reawaken. New centres of power began to form in the provinces, which were already known to be political units. Szechwan, for instance, . . . was one such unit. There was similar pressure for independence from the central government in other provinces, especially in those lying more on the periphery, such as Kwang-tung–Kwangsi, Yunnan, Kansu, Shensi, etc. The dependencies of Tibet, Sinkiang, Mongolia and Manchuria established *de facto* independence soon after 1911. The revolution led to a period of constant internal conflicts, in which regional factors often played at least as important a role as ideological factors, if not more so. This was one of the main reasons why Sun Yat-sen resigned the Presidency; he realized he would not be able to hold the country together. Those who controlled the central and southern provinces would have recognized his Presidency—at least *de jure*—but not the provinces of the North. Yüan Shih-k'ai seemed to be the only one of whom it could be hoped that he would be able to preserve the unity of the Empire. He succeeded only in part; his Presidency was the prelude to the period of the great civil wars. Thus, the overthrow of the monarchy which meant a revolution of the constitution was the prelude to the serious disturbances and consequent suffering which China was to experience in the following decades.

THE BEGINNINGS OF THE REPUBLIC

It was primarily the organization and initiative of the Revolutionary Alliance under the leadership of Sun Yat-sen that led to the formation in 1911 of a broad, united revolutionary front which was successful in getting the Ch'ing dynasty to abdicate and in establishing the Republic. But the united front came to an end with this success, and it soon became clear that the numerous different forces which had been united by the common aim of overthrowing Manchu rule were pulling against one another again once their first aim had been achieved. New fronts which were hostile to one another soon formed. Thus, the overthrow of the ruling dynasty by the revolution of 1911 shows largely the same features as similar events in the past. Even so the characteristics of the peasant revolt do not stand out: it is much more like the frequent military insurrections against the ruling dynasty in the past. In 1911, of course—as not infrequently before—both elements are to be found, but the latter was clearly predominant. These traditional elements in the form of the revolution do not exclude its deeper significance, which we tried to characterize in the last section as something completely new, without parallel in Chinese history.

When Sun Yat-sen resigned his acting presidency in favour of Yüan Shih-k'ai in February, 1912, he relied on Yüan to make the cause of the revolution and the republic his own. This trust says much for Sun's idealism and optimism, but not for his knowledge of human nature or his judgment of the real situation. His expectations were soon disappointed. Yüan Shih-k'ai enjoyed the trust of the military as well as the Revolutionary Alliance. He was regarded as the only person who could possibly control the new and difficult situation. The provisional government of the revolutionaries had established itself in Nanking and in deliberate imitation of the first rulers of the Ming dynasty it had decided to make Nanking the capital of China once more. It was decided to remove the republican capital from the atmosphere of Peking at the very beginning because Peking combined cultural refinement and traditional modes of life with decadence, intrigue and corruption—in short, all the good and bad features of the old regime. Yüan Shih-k'ai, whose military and political power was based on the North, had his own reasons for not moving the capital to Nanking. As a result of military revolts, which broke out—possibly at his own secret instigation—in Peking and other places in northern China at the very moment when he was due to arrive in Nanking, it was clear that his presence in Peking was absolutely indispensable. Thus despite the annoyance of the more radical revolutionary elements from southern and central China, Peking continued to be the capital.

Reference has already been made to the weakness of these radical revolutionaries. They wanted to introduce ideas and institutions of freedom, constitutional government and democracy from the West where the ethos and structure of society were quite different, into a China for which these ideas and institutions were alien and unsuitable. These ideas and the institutions associated with them were a historical development from western civilization and had been able to develop successfully only in the West. The Chinese revolutionaries, who were full of Western ideas, spoke a language that was to a certain extent foreign to their own countrymen, and they were not understood. Apart from Sun Yat-sen and a number of other idealists, who were genuinely seeking the best for their country, the revolution had attracted a very mixed group of people, some of whom were only interested in seeking office and in the illegal financial gain which was easily combined with this, or in other personal advantages. Thus, the parliamentary elections, which took place at the beginning of 1913 and which gave the Revolutionary Party—now called the Kuomintang, 'the National Party'—a majority of seats, were a farce. The results were determined almost entirely by bribery and terror. The election issues were not political programmes or convictions but the benefits accruing to individuals and groups, for whom the victory of their party was a vital question financially. By their preparation for the revolution the Kuomintang had built up the most effective and widespread organization. Apart from the centres of the revolutionary movement abroad, the revolution's headquarters in China itself were in the southern province of Kwangtung, especially in the provincial capital of Canton, where Western influences had first found entrance along with Western trade. The provincial government of Kwangtung, which was largely independent of the central government in Peking, consisted largely of the newcomers from the revolutionary movement. An accurate first-hand description of the prevailing spirit in Canton is to be found in a contemporary French observer, who wrote as follows:

> This youthful provincial government was composed of journalists, students from abroad, sons of industrialists, merchants and previously rebellious petty officials. In their eyes the spirit of tradition was the enemy of progress; it was to be attacked in all its forms. They were to teach the opposite of what had been taught in the past and make an absolutely fresh start. The advocates of this theory were not, as one might imagine, ideological philosophers, full of abstractions. At the head of the direction of industry there was to be found an industrialist who had worked for many years in the factories owned by his father-in-law in the South Sea; finance was in the hands of a large merchant from the southern ports. Other branches of the administration were the responsibility of the specialists. Frenchmen wrongly think that the Chinese of the new generation are theoreticians and fanatical disciples of Rousseau and our encyclopaedists; in fact very few of them have read them. The young rulers of Canton are practical men with purely mercantile interests, i.e. utilitarians. They condemned the forms of the old civilization because they seemed to be hindering the economic progress of the

country. They presented the Republican régime as the most suitable framework for commercial and industrial development, a broad, flexible framework which, they thought, would not hold back either the individual or the group. In their opinion the apparatus of government had to be reduced to its simplest form, because social activity was the chief requisite. . . .

Overseas Chinese were noted for their fairly emphatic disregard of government affairs, and they devoted their energies to the questions of exploiting the sources of wealth. These immigrant Chinese may be regarded as displaced persons, who were maimed or deformed by their contact with different cultures. At the same time it should be recognized that they wanted action; they wanted to do something useful; and they were enterprising in outlook. But precisely because they lived abroad, in a cosmopolitan environment, they were hardly aware of forces which were hostile to the renewal of which they dreamed. . . .

These young reformers, who were not dependent on Chinese education, had been particularly subject to the influence of American protestantism and American education. The American citizen was the model for the Chinese of tomorrow. The American's active life, independent, in a world without restrictions, completely dominated by the profit motive, was a very powerful attraction. China's young people were convinced that such a blossoming of human personality was only possible if differences of social hierarchy disappeared and privileges and prerogatives of class were unknown. The first and most important lesson was that there should be equality of opportunity; prejudices and received opinions, family and other ties must be abolished, in order that the individual might be free to engage in the struggle for wealth.[1]

Because of tendencies such as those described above the revolution of 1911 has been called the 'bourgeois revolution.' These bourgeois elements existed not only in Canton but also in other seaports and they spread considerably in the following period. They also had a certain amount of influence in many local government offices. They were only one element, however, and by no means the most decisive, in the revolution of 1911, so that it hardly seems justifiable to refer to it as 'bourgeois.'

Bourgeois elements did not have as great a share in the revolution, especially in the provinces of the West and South, as the regional forces represented by local gentry or merchants and artisans, who were chiefly concerned not about the choice between monarchy or republic, but about being as little dependent as possible on the central government and paying as little as possible in taxes to the capital. The dispute over the nationalization of the railways, for instance, had revealed not only the existence of such tendencies but also their parallelism with the trends of the revolution. Administration under the Ch'ing dynasty had been strongly centripetal. By stipulating that no one should hold a leading official position in the government of his own province or of his own prefecture or county, regional interests were largely eliminated. This regulation was immediately abolished by the Provisional Government, partly perhaps for purely idealistic and theoretical considerations of local self-administration—which had existed for many years alongside official government agencies in many branches of the administration—without regard for the practical consequences. In addition the regional forces may also have made their fateful influence felt in order to advance their own interests. The abolition of this regulation meant that the road was clear for regional forces, and the break-up of the state's cohesion in the following decades was the inevitable result. Yüan Shih-k'ai, in contrast to the revolutionaries, sought to follow the centralizing tradition of the Manchu government and later reintroduced the relevant regulation of the Ch'ing period. He was not in a position, however, to see that it was implemented everywhere, because of the power which regional forces had already regained.

The revolution and the collapse of the imperial government rendered the position of the prefects and magistrates largely impossible, in so far as they were not taken over and protected by the new holders of power. Newly dispatched prefects and magistrates were usually unqualified and inexperienced and consequently were not usually in a position to enforce their orders. Not infrequently they were attacked and driven from their area of office, if they did not have sufficient military protection. This was often the case in the southwestern provinces particularly. The *de facto* government of a prefecture or a district then fell into the hands of the local notables, who generally belonged to the local gentry, and not infrequently of the leaders in the secret societies, especially the Society of the Elders and Brothers. They were aware only of the interests of their own small regions and were often independent, in practice if not in theory, not only of central government in the capital but also of the provincial government in the provincial capital. This is the reason why in a province like Szechwan, for instance, which at the beginning of the century was one of the best governed and most orderly in the whole country, the mismanagement and caprice of the local holders of power after the revolution assumed increasingly worse forms and the general insecurity constantly increased. These regional forces in the South and West had sided on the whole with the revolutionaries, since they looked to this quarter for protection against the centralizing efforts of Yüan Shih-k'ai and the North.

The new 'republic' was characterized not only by increasing decentralization and the breakaway of provinces from the central government but also by the retreat of the civil power in the face of the military. In the classical Chinese state civil and military power stood side by side. Normally the civil power was predominant, and in theory, at any rate, was always so. The president and the officials of the Ministry of War were always civil officials as well as the provincial governors and governors general who were particularly influential in recent centuries. Civil officials were often entrusted with military tasks. Even in the event of war the executive power remained, theoretically at least, in the hands of the civil authorities. Of course, this did not prevent the government of particular regions or even the whole country being assumed by the army and its leaders in times of unrest. Several of the founders of new dynasties were originally rebel military leaders; however, they always restored the power of the government to the civil authorities as soon as they assumed control.

What followed the revolution of 1911 was somewhat different. Yüan Shih-k'ai was a general and his power rested chiefly on his military strength; three of his four successors as presidents before 1927 were also war-lords. Military leaders often acted in a civil capacity at the same time; in the provinces the military leaders were often simultaneously provincial governors and their subordinates were not infrequently prefects and magistrates. The civil authorities were usually helpless in the face of the army and could not maintain their position without their protection.

It only remains to mention the role played by the great mass of the people, particularly the peasants, in the revolution and the early years of the republic. Apart from the collaboration of the secret societies in central and southern China in the revolution of 1911, the role of the great mass of the population was purely passive. Politics continued to be the preserve of a very small group, and the great majority of the people was not concerned with the revolution and the republic. For the time being, at any rate, the traditional social structure continued almost unaltered. It was only very slowly that the new ideas and the new patterns of life and economics, which were to destroy the traditional order, began to penetrate the Chinese people; but the effect of these new patterns was all the more continuous and lasting. This process of the disintegration of the traditional order has not yet been concluded. The revolution resulting in the overthrow of the monarchy inaugurated this process and this is the reason for the particular importance ascribed to this event.

NOTE

1. Translated from Albert Maybon, *La République Chinoise,* Paris, 1914, pp. 171–5.

CH'EN TU-HSIU
Call to Youth

Ch'en Tu-hsiu (1879–1942), who had studied in Japan and France and taken part in the 1911 Revolution, founded the *Hsin Ch'ing-nien (New Youth)* magazine in Shanghai in 1915. From then on Ch'en became one of the most influential writers in China and his magazine played an exceedingly important role in spreading ideas of social change.

The following article, published in 1915, is an open attack on Confucianism and a stirring call to youth to discard "the old and the rotten" in traditional culture which subordinated the young to the old and the individual to the family. The six principles enunciated by Ch'en are based on Western ideas and are meant to serve as a model to be followed by the "new" youth of resurgent China. The tyranny of tradition had to be broken before true freedom and democracy could find roots in China.

The Chinese compliment others by saying, "He acts like an old man although still young." Englishmen and Americans encourage one another by saying, "Keep young while growing old." Such is one respect in which the different ways of thought of the East and West are

Reprinted by permission of the publishers from Ssu-yü Teng and John K. Fairbank, *China's Response to the West: A Documentary Survey 1839–1923,* pp. 240–246. Cambridge, Mass.: Harvard University Press, Copyright, 1954, by the President and Fellows of Harvard College.

manifested. Youth is like early spring, like the rising sun, like trees and grass in bud, like a newly sharpened blade. It is the most valuable period of life. The function of youth in society is the same as that of a fresh and vital cell in a human body. In the process of metabolism, the old and the rotten are incessantly eliminated to be replaced by the fresh and living. . . . If metabolism functions properly in a human body, the person will be healthy; if the old and rotten cells accumulate and fill the body, the person will die. If metabolism functions properly in a society, it will flourish; if old and rotten elements fill the society, then it will cease to exist.

According to this standard, then, is the society of our nation flourishing, or is it about to perish? I cannot bear to answer. As for those old and rotten elements, I shall leave them to the process of natural selection. I do not wish to waste my fleeting time in arguing with them on this and that and hoping for them to be reborn and thoroughly remodeled. I only, with tears, place my plea before the young and vital youth, in the hope that they will achieve self-awareness, and begin to struggle. What is this self-awareness? It is to be conscious of the value and responsibility of one's young life and vitality, to maintain one's self-respect, which should not be lowered. What is the struggle? It is to exert one's intellect, discard resolutely the old and the rotten, regard them as enemies and as the flood or savage beasts, keep away from their neighborhood and refuse to be contaminated by their poisonous germs. Alas! Do these words really fit the youth of our country? I have seen that, out of every ten youths who are young in age, five are old in physique; and out of every ten who are young in both age and physique, nine are old in mentality. Those with shining hair, smooth countenance, a straight back and a wide chest are indeed magnificent youths! Yet if you ask what thoughts and aims are entertained in their heads, then they all turn out to be the same as the old and rotten, like moles from the same hill. In the beginning the youth are not without freshness and vitality. Gradually some are assimilated by the old and rotten elements; then there are others who fear the tremendous influence of those elements, who hesitate, stammer and stall, and dare not openly rebel against them. It is the old and rotten air that fills society everywhere. One cannot even find a bit of fresh and vital air to comfort those of us who are suffocating in despair.

Such a phenomenon, if found in a human body, would kill a man; if found in a society, would destroy it. A heavy sigh or two cannot cure this malady. What is needed is for one or two youths, who are quick in self-consciousness and brave in a struggle, to use to the full the natural intellect of man, and judge and choose all the thoughts of mankind, distinguishing which are fresh and vital and suitable for the present struggle for survival, and which are old and rotten and unworthy to be retained in the mind. Treat this problem as a sharp tool cleaves iron, or a sharp knife cuts hemp. Resolutely make no compromises and entertain no hesitations. Consider yourself and consider others; then perhaps society can hope to become clean and peaceful. O youth, is there anyone who takes upon himself such responsibilities? As for understanding what is right and wrong, in order that you may make your choice, I carefully propose the following six principles, and hope you will give them your calm consideration.

1. Be independent, not servile   All men are equal. Each has his right to be independent, but absolutely no right to enslave others nor any obligation to make himself servile. By slavery we mean that in ancient times the ignorant and the weak lost their right of freedom, which was savagely usurped by tyrants. Since the rise of the theories of the rights of man and of equality, no red-blooded person can endure [the name of slave]. The history of modern Europe is commonly referred to as a "history of emancipation": the destruction of monarchical power aimed at political emancipation; the denial of Church authority aimed at religious emancipation; the rise of the theory of equal property aimed at economic emancipation; and the suffragist movement aimed at emancipation from male authority.

Emancipation means freeing oneself from the bondage of slavery and achieving a completely independent and free personality. I have hands and feet, and I can earn my own living. I have a mouth and a tongue, and I can voice my own likes and dislikes. I have a mind, and I can determine my own beliefs. I will absolutely not let others do these things in my behalf, nor should I assume an overlordship and enslave others. For once the independent personality is recognized, all matters of conduct, all rights and privileges, and all belief should be left to the natural ability of each person; there is definitely no reason why one should blindly follow others. On the other hand, loyalty, filial piety, chastity and righteousness are a slavish morality. (Note: The great German philosopher Nietzsche divided morality into two categories—that which is independent and courageous is called "morality of the noble," and that which is humble and submissive is called "morality of the slave.") Light penalties and light taxation constitute the happiness of slaves; panegyrics and eulogies are slavish literature;

. . . noble ranks or magnificent mansions are glory only to slaves; resplendent tablets and grand tombs are their memorials. That is because such persons, by submitting to the judgment of others regarding right and wrong, glory and shame, instead of depending on their own standard of judgment, have completely annihilated their independent and equal personalities as individuals. In their conduct, whether good or bad, they cannot appeal to their own will-power, but are confined to receiving merits or demerits (from others). Who can say that it is improper to call such persons slaves? Therefore, before we speak of contributing to mankind in moral example or in deed, we must first make this distinction between the independent and the servile.

2. Be progressive, not conservative   "Without progress there will be retrogression" is an old Chinese saying. Considering the fundamental laws of the universe, all things or phenomena are daily progressing in evolution, and the maintenance of the *status quo* is definitely out of the question; only the limitation of man's ordinary view has rendered possible the differentiation between the two states of things. This is why the theory of creative evolution, "L'Evolution créatrice," of the contemporary French philosopher Henri Bergson, has become immensely popular throughout a whole generation. Considered in the light of the evolution of human affairs, it is plain that those races that cling to antiquated ways are declining, or disappearing, day by day, and the peoples who seek progress and advancement are just beginning to ascend in power and strength. It is possible to predict which of these will survive and which will not. Now our country still has not awakened from its long dream, and isolates itself by going down the old rut. . . . All our traditional ethics, law, scholarship, rites and customs are survivals of feudalism. When compared with the achievement of the white race, there is a difference of a thousand years in thought, although we live in the same period. Revering only the history of the twenty-four dynasties and making no plans for progress and improvement, our people will be turned out of this twentieth-century world, and be lodged in the dark ditches fit only for slaves, cattle, and horses. What more need be said? I really do not know what sort of institutions and culture are adequate for our survival in the present world if in such circumstances conservatism is still advocated. I would much rather see the past culture of our nation disappear than see our race die out now because of its unfitness for living in the modern world. Alas, the days of the Babylonians are past. Of what use is their civilization now? "When the skin has vanished, what can the hair adhere to?" The progress of the world is like that of a fleet horse, galloping and galloping onward. Whatever cannot skillfully change itself and progress along with the world will find itself eliminated by natural-selection because of failure to adapt to the environment. Then what can be said to defend conservatism!

3. Be aggressive, not retiring While the tide of evil is now rushing onward, would it not be rare virtue for one or two self-respecting scholars to retire from the world, to keep themselves clean? But if your aim is to influence the people and establish a new tradition, I suggest that you make further progress from your present high position. It is impossible to avoid the struggle for survival, and so long as one draws breath there can be no place where one can retire for a tranquil hermit's life. It is our natural obligation in life to advance in spite of numerous difficulties. Stated in kindly terms, retirement is an action of the superior man in order to get away from the vulgar world. Stated in hostile terms, it is a phenomenon of the weak who are unable to struggle for survival. . . . Alas! The war steeds of Europe are intruding into your house. Where can you quietly repose under a white cloud? I wish that our youth would become Confucius and Mo-tzu and not [the hermits] Ts'ao-fu and Hsü Yu,[1] and I do not wish so much that your youth be Tolstoi and Tagore (Note: R. Tagore, an escapist poet of India) as that they become Columbus and An Ch'ung-ken [the Korean patriot who assassinated Prince Ito on October 26, 1909].

4. Be cosmopolitan, not isolationist Any change in the economic or political life of one nation will usually have repercussions over the whole world, just as the whole body is affected when one hair is pulled. The prosperity or decline, rise or fall of a nation today depends half on domestic administration, and half on influences from outside the country. Take the recent events of our country as evidence: Japan suddenly rose in power, and stimulated our revolutionary and reform movements; the European War broke out, and then Japan presented her demands to us; is this not clear proof? When a nation is thrown into the currents of the world, traditionalists will certainly hasten the day of its fall, but those capable of change will take this opportunity to compete and progress. According to the pessimists, since the opening of the treaty ports our country has been losing territory and paying indemnities to the point of exhaustion. But according to the optimists, we would still be in the age of the eight-legged essay and the queue were it not for the blessings of the Sino-Japanese War of 1895 and the Boxer Uprising of

1900. Not only are we unable to support an isolationist and closed-door policy, but circumstances also are unfavorable to it. . . . If at this point one still raises a particularist theory of history and of national circumstances and hopes thereby to resist the current, then this still indicates the spirit of an isolationist country and a lack of knowledge of the world. When its citizens lack knowledge of the world, how can a nation expect to survive in it? A proverb says, "He who builds his cart behind closed gates will find it not suited to the tracks outside the gates." The cart-builders of today not only close their gates, but even want to use the methods contained in the chapter on technology in the *Rites of Chou* for use on the highways of Europe and America. The trouble will be more than not fitting the tracks.

5. Be utilitarian, not formalistic   The social system and the thought of Europe have undergone a change since J. S. Mill's advocacy of utilitarianism in England and Comte's advocacy of positivism in France. More recently their system and thought have undergone another change, with the great advancement of science in Germany, where material civilization has reached its pinnacle of achievement. In all that concerns the administration of government, the aims of education, and the fashions in literature and the crafts, there is nothing that is not focusing on the road of better livelihood and greater usefulness, like ten thousand horses galloping toward the same point. Meanwhile all things that are formalistic, utopian, and useless to practical life are almost completely rejected. The great comtemporary philosophers, such as R. Eucken of Germany and Bergson of France, although they do not consider the present materialistic civilization perfect, all discuss the problems of life (Note: The English word is "life," the German "leben," and the French "la vie") as the goal of their teachings. Life is sacred. Because the blood of the present war has stained life's bright banner, the Europeans will waken entirely from utopian, empty dreams.

Generally speaking, concern for usefulness and better livelihood, respect for actuality and disdain for illusion were characteristic of the ancient people of our country, whereas our present social system and thought are inherited from the Chou and Han dynasties. Empty formalism was emphasized in the *Rites of Chou,* and under the Han dynasty Confucianism and the Taoism of Lao-tzu were elevated to high positions, while all other schools of thought were interdicted. The age-long precepts of ethical convention, the hopes and purposes of the people—there is nothing which does not run counter to the practical life of society today. If we do not restring our bow and renew our effort, there will be no way to revive the strength of our nation, and our society will never see a peaceful day. As for praying to gods to relieve flood and famine, or reciting the *Book of Filial Piety* to ward off the Yellow Turbans [i.e., bandits]—people are not infants or morons, and they see through these absurdities. Though a thing is of gold or of jade, if it is of no practical use, then it is of less value than coarse cloth, grain, manure or dirt. That which brings no benefit to the practical life of an individual or of society is all empty formalism and the stuff of cheats. And even though it were bequeathed to us by our ancestors, taught by the sages, advocated by the government and worshiped by society, the stuff of cheats is still not worth one cent.

6. Be scientific, not imaginative What is science? It is our general conception of matter which, being the sum of objective phenomena as analyzed by subjective reason, contains no contradiction within itself. What is imagination? It first oversteps the realm of objective phenomena, and then discards reason itself; it is something constructed out of thin air, consisting of hypotheses without proof, and all the existing wisdom of mankind cannot be made to find reason in it or explain its laws and principles. There was only imagination and no science in the unenlightened days of old, as well as among the uncivilized peoples of today. Religion, art, and literature were the products of the period of imagination. The contribution of the growth of science to the supremacy of modern Europe over other races is not less than that of the theory of the rights of man. . . . Our scholars do not know science, therefore they borrow the *yin-yang* school's notions of auspicious signs and of the five elements to confuse the world and cheat the people, and the ideas of topography and geomancy to beg for miracles from dry skeletons (spirits). Our farmers do not know science; therefore they have no technique for seed selection and insecticide. Our industrialists do not know science; therefore goods lie wasted on the ground, while we depend on foreign countries for everything that we need in warfare and in production. Our merchants know no science; therefore they are only concerned with obtaining short-term profits, and give not a thought to calculating for the future. Our physicians know no science; not only are they not acquainted with human anatomy, but also they do not analyze the properties of medicines; as for bacteria and contagious diseases, they have never heard of them. They can only parrot the talk about the five elements, their mutual promotions and preventions, cold and heat, *yin* and *yang,* and prescribe medicine according to ancient formulae. Their technique is practically the same as that of an archer! The height of their marvelous imaginations is the theory of *chi* (primal force), which even extends to the techniques of professional strong men and Taoist priests. But though you seek high and low in the universe, you will never know what this "primal force" exactly is. All these nonsensical ideas and unreasonable beliefs can be cured at the root only by science. For to explain truth by science means proving everything with fact. Although the process is slower than that of imagination and arbitrary decision, yet every step taken is on firm ground; it is different from those imaginative flights which eventually cannot advance even one inch. The amount of truth in the universe is boundless, and the fertile areas in the realm of science awaiting the pioneer are immense! Youth, take up the task!

NOTE

1. According to legend, Ts'ao-fu and Hsü Yu both refused to accept the throne when the Emperor Yao offered it to them successively, thus showing their utter contempt for worldly glory.

HU SHIH
The Literary Revolution

Along with the attacks on Confucian ideas and values came an attack on the classical literary language which was not only the language of tradition but, because of its difficult nature, had also helped to maintain the gap between the privileged scholar elite and the masses.

In the following article,[1] published in *New Youth* in January 1917, Hu Shih (1891–1962), who was then a student in the United States, put forward an eight-point program for literary reform. This was the beginning of the "literary revolution" which displaced the classical literary language for the vernacular *(pai-hua)* and had a far-reaching effect on the course of the Chinese Revolution. The vernacular was a better means of communication for reaching more people on modern issues, and acceptance of the vernacular as respectable opened

From Wm. Theodore deBary, ed., *Sources of Chinese Tradition* (New York: Columbia University Press, 1960), pp. 820–824. Reprinted by permission.

the way for younger writers to express their deepest feelings more freely than ever before.

Many people have been discussing literary reform. Who am I, unlearned and unlettered, to offer an opinion? Nevertheless, for some years I have studied the matter and thought it over many times, helped by my deliberations with friends; and the conclusions I have come to are perhaps not unworthy of discussion. Therefore I shall summarize my views under eight points and elaborate on them separately to invite the study and comments of those interested in literary reform.

I believe that literary reform at the present time must begin with these eight items: 1. Write with substance; 2. Do not imitate the ancients; 3. Emphasize grammar; 4. Reject melancholy; 5. Eliminate old clichés; 6. Do not use allusions; 7. Do not use couplets and parallelisms; and 8. Do not avoid popular expressions or popular forms of characters.

1. Write with substance. By "substance" I mean: (a) Feeling . . . Feeling is the soul of literature. Literature without feeling is like a man without a soul. . . . (b) Thought. By thought I mean insight, knowledge, and ideals. Thought does not necessarily depend on literature for transmission but literature becomes more valuable if it contains thought, and thought is more valuable if it possesses literary value. This is the reason why the essays of Chuang Tzu, the poems of T'ao Ch'ien [365–427], Li Po [689–762], and Tu Fu [712–770], the *tz'u* of Hsin Chia-hsüan [1140–1207], and the novel of Shih Nai-an [that is, the *Shui-hu chuan* or *Water Margin*] are matchless for all times. . . . In recent years literary men have satisfied themselves with tones, rhythm, words, and phrases, and have had neither lofty thoughts nor genuine feeling. This is the chief cause of the deterioration of literature. This is the bad effect of superficiality over substantiality, that is to say, writing without substance. To remedy this bad situation, we must resort to substance. And what is substance? Nothing but feeling and thought.

2. Do not imitate the ancients. Literature changes with time. Each period from Chou and Ch'in to Sung, Yüan, and Ming has its own literature. This is not my private opinion but the universal law of the advancement of civilization. Take prose, for example. There is the prose of the *Book of History,* the prose of the ancient philosophers, the prose of [the historians] Ssu-ma Ch'ien and Pan Ku, the prose of the [T'ang and Sung masters] Han Yü, Liu Tsung-yüan, Ou-yang Hsiu, and

Su Hsün, the prose of the *Recorded Conversations* of the Neo-Confucianists, and the prose of Shih Nai-an and Ts'ao Hsüeh-ch'in [d. c.1765, author of *The Dream of the Red Chamber*]. This is the development of prose. . . . Each period has changed in accordance with its situation and circumstance, each with its own characteristic merits. From the point of view of historical evolution, we cannot say that the writings of the ancients are all superior to those of modern writers. The prose of Tso Ch'iu-ming [sixth century B.C., author of the *Tso chuan*] and Ssu-ma Ch'ien are wonderful, but compared to the *Tso chuan* and *Records of the Historian,* wherein is Shih Nai-an's *Shui-hu chuan* inferior? . . .

I have always held that colloquial stories alone in modern Chinese literature can proudly be compared with the first class literature of the world. Because they do not imitate the past but only describe the society of the day, they have become genuine literature. . . .

3. Emphasize grammar. Many writers of prose and poetry today neglect grammatical construction. Examples are too numerous to mention, especially in parallel prose and the four-line and eight-line verses.

4. Reject melancholy. This is not an easy task. Nowadays young writers often show passion. They choose such names as "Cold Ash," "No Birth," and "Dead Ash" as pen names, and in their prose and poetry, they think of declining years when they face the setting sun, and of destitution when they meet the autumn wind. . . . I am not unaware of the fact that our country is facing many troubles. But can salvation be achieved through tears? I hope all writers become Fichtes and Mazzinis and not like Chia I [201–169 B.C.], Wang Ts'an [177–217], Ch'ü Yüan [343–277 B.C.], Hsieh Kao-yü [1249–1295], etc. [who moaned and complained]. . . .

5. Eliminate old clichés. By this I merely mean that writers should describe in their own words what they personally experience. So long as they achieve the goal of describing the things and expressing the mood without sacrificing realism, that is literary achievement. Those who employ old clichés are lazy people who refuse to coin their own terms of description.

6. Do not use allusions. I do not mean allusion in the broad sense. These are of five kinds: (a) Analogies employed by ancient writers, which have a universal meaning . . . ; (b) Idioms; (c) References to historical events . . . ; (d) Quoting from or referring to people in the past for comparison . . . ; and (e) Quotations. . . . Allusions such as these may or may not be used.

But I do not approve of the use of allusions in the narrow sense. By using allusions I mean that writers are incapable of creating their own expressions to portray the scene before them or the concepts in their minds, and instead muddle along by borrowing old stories or expressions which are partly or wholly inapplicable. . . .

7. Do not use couplets and parallelisms. Parallelism is a special characteristic of human language. This is why in ancient writings such as those of Lao Tzu and Confucius, there are occasionally couplets. The first chapter of the *Tao-te ching* consists of three couplets. *Analects* I:14, I:15 and III:17 are all couplets. But these are fairly natural expressions and have no indication of being forced or artificial, especially because there is no rigid requirement about the number of words, tones, or parts of speech. Writers in the age of literary decadence, however, who had nothing to say, emphasized superficiality, the extreme of which led to the development of the parallel prose, regulated *tz'u,* and the long regulated verse. It is not that there are no good products in these forms, but they are, in the final analysis, few. Why? Is it not because they restrict to the highest degree the free expression of man? (Not a single good piece can be mentioned among the long regulated verse.) To talk about literary reform today, we must "first establish the fundamental"[2] and not waste our useful energy in the nonessentials of subtlety and delicacy. This is why I advocate giving up couplets and rhymes. Even if they cannot be abolished, they should be regarded as merely literary stunts and nothing to be pursued seriously.

There are still people today who deprecate colloquial novels as trifling literature, without realizing that Shih Nai-an, Ts'ao Hsüeh-ch'in, and Wu Chien-jen [1867–1910][3] all represent the main line of literature while parallel and regulated verse are really trifling matters. I know some will keep clear of me when they hear this.

8. Do not avoid popular expressions or popular forms of characters. When Buddhist scriptures were introduced into China, because classical expressions could not express their meanings, translators used clear and simple expressions. Their style already approached the colloquial. Later, many Buddhist lectures and dialogues were in the colloquial style, thus giving rise to the "conversation" style. When the Neo-Confucianists of the Sung dynasty used the colloquial in their *Recorded Conversations,* this style became the orthodox style of scholarly discussion. (This was followed by scholars of the Ming.) By that time, colloquial expressions had already penetrated rhymed prose, as can be seen in the colloquial poems of T'ang and Sung poets. From the third century to the end of the Yüan, North China had been under foreign races and popular literature developed. In prose there were such novels as the *Shui-hu chuan* and *Hsi yu chi (Journey to the West).* In drama the products were innumerable. From the modern point of view, the Yüan period should be considered as a high point of literary development; unquestionably it produced the greatest number of immortal works. At that time writing and colloquial speech were the closest to each other and the latter almost became the language of literature. Had the tendency not been checked, living literature would have emerged in China, and the great work of Dante and Luther [who inaugurated the substitution of living language for dead Latin] would have taken place in China. Unfortunately, the tendency was checked in the Ming when the government selected officials on the basis of the rigid "eight-legged" prose style and at the same time literary men like the "seven scholars" including Li [Meng-yang, 1472–1529] considered "returning to the past" as highbrow. Thus the once-in-a-millennium chance of uniting writing and speech was killed prematurely, midway in the process. But from the modern viewpoint of historical evolution, we can definitely say that the colloquial literature is the main line of Chinese literature and that it should be the medium employed in the literature of the future. (This is my own opinion; not many will agree with me today.) For this reason, I hold that we should use popular expressions and words in prose and poetry. Rather than using dead expressions of 3,000 years ago, it is better to employ living expressions of the twentieth century, and rather than using the language of the Ch'in, Han, and the Six Dynasties, which cannot reach many people and cannot be universally understood, it is better to use the language of the *Shui-hu* and *Hsi yu chi* which is understood in every household.

NOTES

1. *A Preliminary Discussion of Literary Reform.* From *Wen-hsüeh kai-liang ch'un* in *Hu Shih wen-ts'un,* Collection I, Ch. 1. pp. 5–16; original version in *Hsin ch'ing-nien,* Vol.II, No.5 (January 1917), pp. 1–11.

2. *Mencius*, VI, A:15.
3. Author of the *Erh-shih nien mu-tu chih kuai hsien-chuang (Strange Phenomena Seen in Two Decades)*.

LU HSÜN
A Madman's Diary

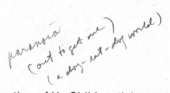

In 1918, a year following the publication of Hu Shih's article quoted in the last reading, *New Youth* came out entirely in the vernacular. It was also in 1918 that China's outstanding representative of modern literature, Lu Hsün (1881–1936) wrote his first story, "A Madman's Diary," in *pai-hua*. The story embodies the two new trends of this revolutionary age: it is written in *pai-hua,* and it attacks the oppressive and exploitative nature of Confucianism which had fostered a "man-eating" society behind a cloak of lofty concepts of ethics and morality. Modern Chinese literature, which dates from this period, made an important contribution to the Chinese Revolution.

Lu Hsün went to Japan in 1902, and there he studied Western medicine, philosophy and literature. The exposure to Western thought and Japanese nationalism made him an ardent revolutionary. He gave up medicine for literature because he felt that China needed a "change of spirit" and that literature could help promote a new culture.

Two brothers, whose names I need not mention here, were both good friends of mine in high school; but after a separation of many years we gradually lost touch. Some time ago I happened to hear that one of them was seriously ill, and since I was going back to my old home I broke my journey to call on them. I saw only one of them, however, who told me that the invalid was his younger brother.

"I appreciate your coming such a long way to see us," he said, "but he recovered some time ago and has gone elsewhere to take up an official post." Then, laughing, he produced two volumes of his

From *Selected Works of Lu Hsün* (Peking: Foreign Languages Press, 1956), pp. 8–21.

brother's diary, saying that from these the nature of his past illness could be seen, and that there was no harm in showing them to an old friend. I took the diary away and read it through, and found that he had suffered from a form of persecution complex. The writing was most confused and incoherent, and he had made many wild statements; moreover he had omitted to give any dates, so that only by the colour of the ink and the differences in the writing could one tell that it was not written at one time. Certain sections, however, were not altogether disconnected, and I have copied out a part to serve as a subject for medical research. I have not altered a single illogicality in the diary and have changed only the names, even though the people referred to are all country folk, unknown to the world and of no consequence. As for the title, it was chosen by the diarist himself after his recovery, and I did not change it.

Tonight the moon is very bright.

I have not seen it for over thirty years, so today when I saw it I felt in unusually high spirits. I begin to realize that during the past thirty odd years I have been in the dark; but now I must be extremely careful. Otherwise why should that dog at the Chao house have looked at me twice?

I have reason for my fear.

Tonight there is no moon at all, I know that this bodes ill. This morning when I went out cautiously, Mr. Chao had a strange look in his eyes, as if he were afraid of me, as if he wanted to murder me. There were also seven or eight others, who discussed me in a whisper. And they were afraid of my seeing them. All the people I passed were like that. The fiercest among them grinned at me; whereupon I shivered from head to foot, knowing that their preparations were complete.

I was not afraid, however, but continued on my way. A group of children in front were also discussing me, and the look in their eyes was just like that in Mr. Chao's, while their faces too were ghastly pale. I wondered what grudge these children could have against me to make them behave like this. I could not help calling out: "Tell me!" But then they ran away.

I wonder what grudge Mr. Chao can have against me, what grudge the people on the road can have against me. I can think of nothing except that twenty years ago I trod on Mr. Ku Chiu's[1] account sheets for many years past, and Mr. Ku was very displeased. Although Mr.

Chao does not know him, he must have heard talk of this and decided to avenge him, so he is conspiring with the people on the road against me. But then what of the children? At that time they were not yet born, so why should they have eyed me so strangely today, as if they were afraid of me, as if they wanted to murder me? This really frightens me, it is so bewildering and upsetting.

I know. They must have learnt this from their parents!

I can't sleep at night. Everything requires careful consideration if one is to understand it.

Those people—some of them have been pilloried by the magistrate, some slapped in the face by the local gentry, some have had their wives taken away by bailiffs, some have had their parents driven to suicide by creditors; yet they never looked as frightened and as fierce then as they did yesterday.

The most extraordinary thing was that woman on the street yesterday who was spanking her son and saying, "Little devil! I'd like to bite several mouthfuls out of you to work off my feelings!" Yet all the time she was looking at me. I gave a start, unable to control myself; then all those green-faced, long-toothed people began to laugh derisively. Old Chen hurried forward and dragged me home.

He dragged me home. The folk at home all pretended not to know me; they had the same look in their eyes as all the others. When I went into the study, they locked the door outside as if cooping up a chicken or a duck. This incident left me even more bewildered.

A few days ago a tenant of ours from Wolf Cub Village came to report the failure of the crops, and told my elder brother that a notorious character in their village had been beaten to death; then some people had taken out his heart and liver, fried them in oil and eaten them, as a means of increasing their courage. When I interrupted, the tenant and my brother both stared at me. Only today have I realized that they had exactly the same look in their eyes as those people outside.

Just to think of it sets me shivering from the crown of my head to the soles of me feet.

They eat human beings, so they may eat me.

I see that woman's "bite several mouthfuls out of you," the laughter of those green-faced, long-toothed people and the tenant's story the other day are obviously secret signs. I realize all the poison in their speech, all the daggers in their laughter. Their teeth are white and glistening: they are all man-eaters.

It seems to me, although I am not a bad man, ever since I trod on Mr. Ku's accounts it has been touch-and-go. They seem to have secrets which I cannot guess, and once they are angry they will call anyone a bad character. I remember when my elder brother taught me to write compositions, no matter how good a man was, if I produced arguments to the contrary he would mark that passage to show approval; while if I excused evil-doers, he would say: "Good for you, that shows originality." How can I possibly guess their secret thoughts—especially when they are ready to eat people?

Everything requires careful consideration if one is to understand it. In ancient times, as I recollect, people often ate human beings, but I am rather hazy about it. I tried to look this up, but my history has no chronology, and scrawled all over each page are the words: "Virtue and Morality." Since I could not sleep anyway, I read hard half the night, until I began to see words between the lines, the whole book being filled with the two words—"Eat people."

All these words written in the book, all the words spoken by our tenant, gaze at me strangely with an enigmatic smile.

I too am a man, and they want to eat me!

In the morning I sat quietly for some time. Old Chen brought lunch in: one bowl of vegetables, one bowl of steamed fish. The eyes of the fish were white and hard, and its mouth was open just like those people who want to eat human beings. After a few mouthfuls I could not tell whether the slippery morsels were fish or human flesh, so I brought it all up.

I said, "Old Chen, tell my brother that I am feeling quite suffocated, and want to have a stroll in the garden." Old Chen said nothing but went out, and presently he came back and opened the gate.

I did not move, watching to see how they would treat me, knowing that they certainly would not let me go. Sure enough! My elder brother came slowly out, leading an old man. There was a murderous gleam in his eyes, and fearing that I would see it he lowered his head, stealing glances at me from the side of his spectacles.

"You seem to be very well today," said my brother.

"Yes," said I.

"I have invited Mr. Ho here today," said my brother, "to examine you."

"All right," said I. But actually I know quite well that this old man was the executioner in disguise! He was simply using the pretext of feeling my pulse to see how fat I was; for by so doing he would be given a share of my flesh. Still I was not afraid. Although I do not eat men, my courage is greater than theirs. I held out my two fists, watching what he would do. The old man sat down, closed his eyes, fumbled for some time and remained still for some time; then he opened his shifty eyes and said, "Don't let your imagination run away with you. Rest quietly for a few days, and you will be all right."

Don't let your imagination run away with you! Rest quietly for a few days! When I have grown fat, naturally they will have more to eat; but what good will it do me, or how can it be "all right"? All these people wanting to eat human flesh and at the same time stealthily trying to keep up appearances, not daring to act promptly, really made me nearly die of laughter. I could not help roaring with laughter, I felt so amused. I knew that in this laughter were courage and integrity. Both the old man and my brother turned pale, awed by my courage and integrity.

But just because I am brave they are the more eager to eat me, in order to acquire some of my courage. The old man went out of the gate, but before he had gone far he said to my brother in a low voice, "To be eaten at once!" And my brother nodded. So you are in it too! This stupendous discovery, although it came as a shock, is yet no more than I had expected: the accomplice in eating me is my elder brother!

The eater of human flesh is my elder brother!

I am the younger brother of an eater of human flesh!

I myself will be eaten by others, but none the less I am the younger brother of an eater of human flesh!

These few days I have been thinking again: suppose that old man were not an executioner in disguise, but a real doctor; he would be none the less an eater of human flesh. In that book on herbs, written by his predecessor Li Shih-chen,[2] it is clearly stated that men's flesh can be boiled and eaten; so can he still say that he does not eat men?

As for my elder brother, I have also good reason to suspect him. When he was teaching me, he said with his own lips, "People exchange their sons to eat." And once, in discussing a bad man, he said that not only did he deserve to be killed, he should "have his flesh eaten and his hide slept on."[3] I was still young then, and my heart beat faster for some time. And he was not at all surprised by the story about eating a man's heart and liver that our tenant from Wolf Cub Village told us the other day, but kept nodding his head. He is evidently just as cruel as before. Since it is possible to "exchange sons to eat," then anything can be exchanged, anyone can be eaten. In the past I simply listened to his explanations, and let it go at that; now I know that when he was explaining to me, not only was there human oil at the corner of his lips, but his whole heart was set on eating men.

Pitch dark. I don't know whether it is day or night. The Chao family dog has started barking again.

The fierceness of a lion, the timidity of a rabbit, the craftiness of a fox. . . .

I know their way; they are not willing to kill anyone outright, nor do they dare, for fear of the consequences. So they have all banded together and set traps everywhere, to force me to kill myself. Just look at the behaviour of the men and women in the street a few days ago, and my elder brother's attitude these last few days, it is quite obvious. What they like best is for a man to take off his belt, and hang himself from a beam; for then they can enjoy their heart's desire without being blamed for murder. Naturally that sets them roaring with delighted laughter. On the other hand, if a man is frightened or worried to death, although that makes him rather thin, they still nod in approval.

They will only eat dead flesh! I remember reading somewhere of a hideous beast, with an ugly look in its eye, called "hyena" which often eats dead flesh. Even the largest bones it grinds into fragments and swallows: the mere thought of this is enough to terrify one. Hyenas are related to wolves, and wolves belong to the canine species. The other day the dog in the Chao house looked at me several times; obviously it is in the plot too and has become their accomplice. The old man's eyes were cast down, but how could that deceive me!

The most deplorable is my elder brother. He is also a man, so why is he not afraid, why is he plotting with others to eat me? Is it that when one is used to it he no longer thinks it a crime? Or is it that he has hardened his heart to do something he knows is wrong?

In cursing man-eaters, I shall start with my brother, and in dissuading man-eaters, I shall start with him too.

Actually, such arguments should have convinced them long ago.
. . .

Suddenly someone came in. He was only about twenty years old and I did not see his features very clearly. His face was wreathed in smiles, and when he nodded to me his smile did not seen genuine. Then I asked him: "Is it right to eat human beings?"

Still smiling, he replied, "When there is no famine how can one eat human beings?"

I realized at once, he was one of them; but still I summoned up courage to repeat my question:

"Is it right?"

"What makes you ask such a thing? You really are . . . fond of a joke. . . . It is very fine today."

"It is fine, and the moon is very bright. But I want to ask you: Is it right?"

He looked disconcerted, and muttered: "No. . . . "

"No? Then why do they still do it?"

"What are you talking about?"

"What am I talking about? They are eating men now in Wolf Cub Village, and you can see it written all over the books, in fresh red ink."

His expression changed, and he grew ghastly pale. "It may be so," he said, staring at me. "It has always been like that. . . . "

"Is it right because it has always been like that?"

"I refuse to discuss these things with you. Anyway, you shouldn't talk about it. Whoever talks about it is in the wrong!"

I leapt up and opened my eyes wide, but the man had vanished. I was soaked with perspiration. He was much younger than my elder brother, but even so he was in it. He must have been taught by his parents. And I am afraid he has already taught his son: that is why even the children look at me so fiercely.

Wanting to eat men, at the same time afraid of being eaten themselves, they all look at each other with the deepest suspicion. . . .

How comfortable life would be for them if they could get rid of such obsessions and go to work, walk, eat and sleep at ease. They have only this one step to take. And yet fathers and sons, husbands and wives, brothers, friends, teachers and students, sworn enemies and even strangers, have all joined in this conspiracy, discouraging and preventing each other from taking this step.

Early this morning I went to look for my elder brother. He was standing outside the hall door looking at the sky, when I walked up behind him, stood between him and the door, and with exceptional poise and politeness said to him:

· "Brother, I have something to say to you."

"Well, what is it?" said he, quickly turning towards me and nodding.

"It is very little, but I find it difficult to say. Brother, probably all primitive people ate a little human flesh to begin with. Later, because their outlook changed, some of them stopped, and because they tried to be good they changed into men, changed into real men. But some are still eating—just like reptiles: some have changed into fish, birds, monkeys and finally men; but some do not try to be good, and remain reptiles still. When those who eat men compare themselves with those who do not, how ashamed they must be. Probably much more ashamed than the reptiles before the monkeys.

"In ancient times Yi Ya boiled his son for Chieh and Chou to eat; that is the old story.[4] But actually since the creation of heaven and earth by Pan Ku men have been eating each other, from the time of Yi Ya's son to the time of Hsu Hsi-lin,[5] and from the time of of Hsu Hsi-lin down to the man caught in Wolf Cub Village. Last year they executed a criminal in the city, and a consumptive soaked a piece of bread in his blood and sucked it.[6]

"They want to eat me, and of course you can do nothing about it single-handed; but why should you join them? As man-eaters they are capable of anything. If they eat me, they can eat you as well; members of the same group can still eat each other. But if you will just change your ways immediately, then everyone will have peace. Although this has been going on since time immemorial, today we could make a special effort to be good, and say this can't be done! I'm sure you can say so, brother. The other day when the tenant wanted the rent reduced, you said it couldn't be done."

At first he only smiled cynically, then a murderous gleam came into his eyes, and when I spoke of their secret his face turned pale. Outside the gate stood a group of people, including Mr. Chao and his dog, all craning their necks to peer in. I could not see all their faces, for they seemed to be masked in cloths; some of them looked pale and ghastly still, concealing their laughter. I knew they were one band, all eaters of human flesh. But I also knew that they did not all think alike by any means. Some of them thought that since it had always been so, men should be eaten. Some of them knew that they should not eat men, but still wanted to; and they were afraid people might discover their secret; thus when they heard me they became angry, but they still smiled their cynical, tight-lipped smile.

Suddenly my brother looked furious, and shouted in a loud voice:

"Get out of here, all of you! What is the point of looking at a madman?"

Then I realized part of their cunning. They would never be willing to change their stand, and their plans were all laid; they had stigmatized me as a madman. In future when I was eaten, not only would there be no trouble, but people would probably be grateful to them. When our tenant spoke of the villagers eating a bad character, it was exactly the same device. This is their old trick.

Old Chen came in too, in a great temper, but they could not stop my mouth, I had to speak to those people:

"You should change, change from the bottom of your hearts!" I said. "You must know that in future there will be no place for man-eaters in the world.

"If you don't change, you may all be eaten by each other. Although so many are born, they will be wiped out by the real men, just like wolves killed by the hunters. Just like reptiles!"

Old Chen drove everybody away. My brother had disappeared. Old Chen advised me to go back to my room. The room was pitch dark. The beams and rafters shook above my head. After shaking for some time they grew larger. They piled on top of me.

The weight was so great, I could not move. They meant that I should die. I knew that the weight was false, so I struggled out, covered in perspiration. But I had to say:

"You should change at once, change from the bottom of your hearts! You must know that in future there will be no place for man-eaters in the world. . . ."

The sun does not shine, the door is not opened, every day two meals.

I took up my chopsticks, then thought of my elder brother; I know now how my little sister died: it was all through him. My sister was only five at the time. I can still remember how lovable and pathetic she looked. Mother cried and cried, but he begged her not to cry, probably because he had eaten her himself, and so crying made him feel ashamed. If he had any sense of shame. . . .

My sister was eaten by my brother, but I don't know whether mother realized it or not.

I think mother must have known, but when she was crying she did not say so outright, probably because she thought it proper too. I remember when I was four or five years old, sitting in the cool of the hall, my brother told me that if a man's parents were ill he should cut off a piece of his flesh and boil it for them, if he wanted to be considered a good son; and mother did not contradict him. If one peice could be eaten, obviously so could the whole. And yet just to think of the mourning then still makes my heart bleed; that is the extraordinary thing about it!

I can't bear to think of it.

I have only just realized that I have been living all these years in a place where for four thousand years they have been eating human flesh. My brother had just taken over the charge of the house when our sister died, and he may well have used her flesh in our rice and dishes, making us eat it unwittingly.

It is possible that I ate several pieces of my sister's flesh unwittingly, and now it is my turn. . . .

How can a man like myself, after four thousand years of man-eating history—even though I knew nothing about it at first—ever hope to face real men?

Perhaps there are still children who have not eaten men? Save the children . . .

April 1918.

NOTES

1. Ku Chiu means "Ancient Times." Lu Hsün had in mind the long history of feudal oppression in China.

2. A famous pharmacologist (1518–1593), author of *Pen-tsao-kang-mu*, the *Materia Medica*.

3. These are quotations from the old classic, *Tso Chuan*.

4. According to ancient records, Yi Ya cooked his son and presented him to Duke Huan of Chi who reigned from 685 to 643 B.C. Chieh and Chou were tyrants of an earlier age. The madman has made a mistake here.

5. A revolutionary at the end of the Ching Dynasty (1644–1911), Hsu Hsi-lin was executed in 1907 for assassinating a Manchu official. His heart and liver were eaten.

6. It was believed that human blood cured consumption. Thus after the execution of a criminal, the executioner would sell steamed bread dipped in blood.

JEROME B. GRIEDER*
The May Fourth Movement

By 1917 the center of the great intellectual ferment (indicated by the previous readings in this chapter) had shifted to Peking University where Chancellor Ts'ai Yuan-p'ei collected a brilliant faculty which included Ch'en Tu-hsiu and Hu Shih. Ts'ai courageously defended academic freedom of thought and expression and the university became a forum for heated debates on political and philosophic issues.

It is no wonder that on May 4, 1919, it was the politically conscious Peking University students who led the demonstrations against the provisions of the Treaty of Versailles and Peking's role at Paris, which allowed Japan to retain control of the erstwhile German-leased territory in Shantung. The spirit of protest spread from Peking to other cities and the students were joined by merchants, shop-keepers, and workers in organized demonstrations and boycotts of Japanese goods. A new sense of nationalism came to pervade the country and, as the following reading indicates, the May Fourth Movement can be seen as "the dividing line between tradition and modernity."

On the morning of Sunday, May 4, 1919, some thousands of university and middle-school students swarmed into the streets of Peking to demonstrate—by their presence and by the placards they carried aloft and the slogans they shouted as they marched—their disapproval of the manner in which China had been treated at the Paris Peace Conference and, equally important, their sense of betrayal by their own government, the warlord regime of Tuan Ch'i-jui.

Nowhere more than in China had Wilsonian principles been taken to

From pp. 208–210 of "Communism, Nationalism, and Democracy: The Chinese Intelligentsia and the Chinese Revolution in the 1920's and the 1930's," by Jerome B. Grieder, in *Modern East Asia: Essays in Interpretation*, edited by James B. Crowley, © 1970 by Harcourt Brace Jovanovich, Inc., and reprinted with their permission.

*Jerome B. Grieder is Associate Professor of Asian History at Brown University. He is author of *Hu Shih and the Chinese Renaissance* (Cambridge, Mass.: Harvard University Press, 1970).

heart in the late teens, at least by the small and articulate minority of Chinese whose opinions constituted the "public" opinion of the day. The Chinese had persuaded themselves, moreover, that their token representation on the Allied side in the recently concluded war, and their participation in the peacemaking that followed, must signal the beginning of a new era in Sino-Western relations, an era that would bring to China the long-sought equality of status among nations. It was, of course, an idle hope. The European powers were too mired at Paris in the diplomacy of retribution to pay sufficient attention to the situation in the Pacific; nor was President Wilson prepared to make the Chinese case a test of those very principles that had roused such enthusiasm among Chinese students and intellectuals. The result of this indifference is well known: The Japanese, who had considerately taken over the administration of formerly German-leased territories in Shantung as their major contribution to the Allied victory, found themselves confirmed in this position at Paris. The Chinese were left with only shattered hopes, an overwhelming sense of betrayal, bitter disillusionment with the meaning of Western ideals, and a profound and smoldering anger.

Nonetheless, a new era was dawning for China, not in Paris but closer to home, in Peking and Shanghai and Tientsin and Hankow and the other centers of the disturbances that erupted in May and June of 1919. The students who inscribed, in their own blood in the white-washed walls of university dining halls and dormitories, denunciations of the Japanese, their Western supporters, and their Chinese cohorts, the students who marched through the streets of the ancient capital or who carried the movement into the streets of other cities over the next days and weeks—these were the prototype of a new generation of intellectual and political leadership, the first representatives of a new force in China's revolutionary experience.

It was not the function of intellectual dissent that was new in China but rather its substance and the manner of its expression. Confucian society had always assigned to its intellectual elite—those versed in Confucian literature and sensitive to Confucian standards of right conduct—an important role as critics of the political order. Often this responsibility had been discharged only at the level of symbolic remonstrance, but on occasion criticism of imperial policy had been more forcefully expressed, by individuals or by groups, sometimes with dire consequences for the critics. The "student protest" organized by K'ang Yu-wei and Liang Ch'i-ch'ao among examination candidates gathered in Peking in 1895 had been somewhat in this tradition. But the student protests of 1919 were far different in scope and in intent. The temper of their challenge to authority is less reminiscent of the traditional style of criticism within the accepted limits of a reigning orthodoxy than it is suggestive of the kind of intellectual dissent that has become increasingly familiar the world over in the last half-century. The Chinese students of 1919 proclaimed their lack of confidence in the warlord government of the day. More than this, they denied the legitimacy of any government in which the Chinese people refused to place their confidence. It was this assertion—implied rather than articulated, at the time—that constituted the real impact of the May Fourth experience on later Chinese politics.

The students, of course, regarded themselves as spokesmen for the Chinese people, since the masses were as yet incapable of taking such an initiative themselves. In this sense the intellectual dissenters of the May Fourth period reflected a self-image much in the pattern of earlier Confucian history. To a significant degree, however, the May Fourth movement involved others besides the students. It received substantial support not only from the small urban professional class, largely Western trained—the teachers, journalists, lawyers, engineers, doctors, and technicians who serviced China's growing modern enterprises—but from the urban commercial class, from large manufacturers, and from small shopkeepers, who participated in the movement by supporting the anti-Japanese boycott. The May Fourth movement was the closest thing to a "mass" movement that the Chinese had experienced to that time. And it brought into prominence and temporary alliance social forces that would figure importantly in the tempestuous course of the next three decades: the dissident (if not yet entirely disaffected) younger intelligentsia, the more or less modernized (or Westernized) elements of the urban population, and the commercial bourgeoisie.

In these respects, 1919 appears an even more significant year than 1911. And it is not without cause that Chinese Communist historians are wont to trace the origins of the Communist movement to this period, partly because the May Fourth movement lent impetus to the popularization of Marxist-Leninist social and political analysis—theories that had barely begun to attract an intellectual audience on the eve of the events of 1919—and also because this informal collaboration between discontented intellectuals and nationalistic businessmen foreshadowed the revolutionary strategy later pursued with some success by the Chinese Communists.

CHARLOTTE FURTH*

The Restructuring of the Chinese Consciousness

As the concluding piece to this section we have a selection from Charlotte Furth which is a broad examination of the role of the intelligentsia of the May Fourth era. These men formed an "in-between generation" that had been exposed through early education to traditional culture and ethics and through later education to Western thought and knowledge. Patriotic and nationalistic, the intelligentsia had a genuine desire to help modernize China but it was "torn between angry iconoclasm and nostalgic attachment to a great cultural heritage." The intellectuals wanted to replace China's traditional social inheritance with a "new culture" but they were faced with deciding what Western elements should constitute the "new culture" and how this culture could be made a reality.

China was called a republic for thirty-seven years, from 1912, when the Manchu dynasty finally abdicated, to the victorious Communist revolution of 1949. Since thirty-seven years is little more than half a lifetime, individuals whose active careers were concentrated in that interval were born before the republic came into existence, and many survived long after it was over. The abrupt change and concentrated pace made Republican reformers self-conscious, often frustrated experimentalists, attempting to mold a society still deeply conditioned to the habits of imperial Confucianism. Although Western models dominated reformist thinking, their application met with many obstacles, both inherited from past tradition and imposed by the anarchic conditions of Republican politics.

Yet the failure of the republic as an institutional experiment, however tragic, was stimulating to the intellectual life of the time, creating an atmosphere of dynamic speculation and debate among men freed by

Reprinted by permission of the publishers from pp. 1-5 of Charlotte Furth, *Ting Wen-chiang*, Cambridge, Mass.: Harvard University Press, Copyright 1970 by the President and Fellows of Harvard College.

*Charlotte Furth is Associate Professor of History at California State University at Long Beach.

social chaos from the restraints as well as the comforts of orthodoxy. Because of the historical association of scholarship and power in Confucian China, the intelligentsia who led the way in these debates formed a particularly sensitive group within the Republican leadership. As an educated elite, they stood as heirs to the scholar-bureaucrats of the old empire, and, at the same time, their function as scholars made them pioneers in the study of Western ideas and catalysts of innovation.

marginal men

The position of such men, standing between two worlds, is illustrated on the most basic level by the pattern of their education. Under the republic an intellectual of any importance was not merely a student of Western culture but a graduate of a foreign university. Nevertheless, this generation was also the last certain to have been exposed to the Chinese classics and, more important, to the entire Confucian view of the function of knowledge in society. That view linked the realms of thought and action, teaching men to honor learning as fundamental and to associate knowledge with the right to moral and political leadership. Through the imperial examination system, scholarship led directly to political action, and when politics was presumed to be in the hands of an ethically indoctrinated cultural leadership, educated men felt little sense that there need be any basic antagonism between their own highest values and state power. Thus, although the Chinese graduate of a Western university in the early twentieth century was equipped with the intellectual tools provided by a Western scientific or social-scientific curriculum, he often continued to view the career of an educated man in this Confucian perspective. In return, the Chinese public saw him the same way, as enjoying the status and responsibilities of a successful imperial degree holder.

The fact that advanced education in Western subjects was still acquired abroad had important social consequences. It guaranteed that foreign university degrees were available only to the children of the privileged minority which could afford the expense and that they would be earned in specialized subjects like law, engineering, or medicine, for which China did not yet have an appropriate professional context. Back in China, foreign graduates found it hard to function either as a traditional elite, in the manner suggested by their background, or as effective professional men in the fields of their training. Drawn from families with historical pretensions to social leadership, exposed to the traditional high culture and its values, they nevertheless enjoyed more sophisticated and first-hand experience of Western countries than any Chinese ever had before. It made them more aware of the complexity of the West itself and of the full implications of China's material backwardness, more critical of the Chinese past, and, thus, torn between angry iconoclasm and nostalgic attachment to a great cultural heritage. At the same time it left them oddly isolated from many of the immediate problems of China's peasant masses, not only because of the perennial gulf between the educated and the illiterate, but also because of their novel cosmopolitanism, their urban way of life, and their political weakness. In contrast with earlier scholar generations, Republican intellectuals were becoming a relatively alienated group, concentrated in a few universities, government bureaus, and commercial seaports.[1]

China's "new culture movement" was created by such men. Its ideas were first discussed among Chinese students in Japan in the last years of the dynasty, and it reached its widest audience among the educated vanguard during the republic's first decade. As students themselves and men poised between contrasting civilizations, the movement's leaders saw the irony in their effort to create a "culture" overnight, to develop an entire outlook on the world by conscious selection rather than gradual habituation. Since they were intelligentsia, they found it easiest to be effective where the enterprise was itself academic. The great immediate achievement of the new culture movement was the reform of the literary language, which by 1920 or so made it possible for people to communicate on paper in the words of everyday life, and which laid the foundations for eventual mass literacy. The movement's most sustained practical effort was the prolonged examination, in and out of the academies, of all aspects of Western culture, and the establishment of a new Chinese scholarship, critical of native classical canons and in harmony with contemporary worldwide research.

However, the new culture movement involved more than academic reorientation; it also stood for an idealized, programmatic vision of a new Chinese man and society, and as such it fertilized the increasingly radical political action movements of the day.

The theorists of the new culture assumed that societies develop organically as the expression of certain fundamental "principles"—moral, social, and natural. Thus Confucian society had always been described, and so the new culture was expected to flower when key Western principles had been assimilated by Chinese, whose creative forces would thereby be released. The new culture, like the old, had to begin with a kind of man. The movement exalted Western liberalism, nationalism, democracy, and science, each of which was seen in terms of human attitudes generating them, attitudes now needed to effect the moral rearmament of the Chinese consciousness. Chinese were to become personally emancipated, freed from the restraints of the Confucian family, the subjection of filial piety and arranged marriages, the indignities of footbinding and concubinage—people capable of creative work and with a hope for personal happiness. They were to become filled with a new spirit of modern patriotism, which would mobilize them as citizens to free China from the humiliations of foreign exploitation; they were to become active participants in public affairs so that the nation might enjoy unity and freedom from civil war; and lastly, they were to become filled with the spirit of modern science, which would guarantee the rationality of their thoughts and the economic and technological productivity of their labor.

Technically speaking, the new culture movement was the outburst of only a few years, between approximately 1915 and 1923. Then its classic manifestos were written, and the words "*hsin wen hua*" served as a banner for the entire radical intelligentsia. But the assumptions of the movement had had a longer history: the belief that fundamental cultural change was a prerequisite for successful modernization and that the models should come from the West went back to 1902 and Liang Ch'i-ch'ao's call for a "new people."[2] Moreover, problems raised by these assumptions outlasted the high tide of the movement as well as contributing to schisms within it. What should be one's standard for selection? This and like questions divided all-out "Westernizers" from East-West synthesizers and split pragmatists from ideologues. How could the new culture be made a reality? Here evolutionists who relied on the power of a new education to fertilize the natural growth of modern institutions differed from activists impatient to follow theoretical blueprints and even to wage revolutionary war for the necessary political power. In this way the issues of the new culture movement reverberated through the 1920s and 1930s, contributing to the awakening political consciousness of the Chinese people and to the rise of Communism. Its assumptions fed that persistent strand of modern Chinese thought which has placed the restructuring of the Chinese consciousness, down to the root of moral and social attitudes, at the heart of China's modern revolution.

NOTES

1. Y. C. Wang, *Chinese Intellectuals and the West* (Chapel Hill, N.C., 1966). See especially pp. 156-164 and 168-187. See also Mary Wright, "Pre-Revolutionary Intellectuals of China and Russia," *China Quarterly*, No.6: 175-179 (April-June, 1961).
2. Liang Ch'i-ch'ao, "Hsin min shuo" (A new people), *Yin-ping-shih ho chi*, Vol. 19.

III Socialism, Anti-Imperialism, and the Revolution: 1920s

Before 1917 Chinese intellectuals had paid no attention to Marxism as a possible solution to China's problems. The success of the Russian Revolution, however, proved that a country need not first attain a high level of industrialization and capitalism before it could have a socialist revolution. Soviet Russia now provided an attractive alternative to the Western political models which had so far held the interest of the Chinese intelligentsia. Furthermore, socialist Russia's renunciation of all privileges extorted from China in the past, at a time when the Allied Powers were supporting Japan in its imperialist claims on Shantung, won for Moscow the goodwill of Chinese nationalist elements disillusioned with the West.

The May Fourth intellectuals who turned to a study of Marxism-Leninism found that it not only offered them a scientific explanation of China's backwardness but showed how they could play a historic role in liberating their nation from the twin evils of imperialism and feudalism (warlords). Also Russia willingly provided the material help and know-how which resulted in the establishment of the Chinese Communist Party (CCP) and the reorganization of the Kuomintang (KMT) on Soviet lines. In return Russia insisted on an alliance of these two parties under the leadership of KMT, because China had to go through the "bourgeois democratic nationalist" phase before entering the socialist stage.

The selections below deal with this phase of the revolution and show how Marxism came to China and how Russia tried to guide the Chinese Revolution.

BENJAMIN I. SCHWARTZ*
The Origins of Marxism-Leninism in China

The following reading explains how Marxism-Leninism became the new-found faith of some important Chinese intellectuals of the May Fourth period. It is interesting to note that though Ch'en Tu-hsiu and Li Ta-chao (founders of the Chinese Communist Party) had both been advocates of liberal democracy, they, like a majority of Chinese intellectuals, had a predilection for an all-embracing and an instant solution to China's problems. The attraction of Marxism-Leninism lay not only in its messianic message, but in the fact that it provided a blueprint for political action.

In tracing the origins of Marxism-Leninism in China, I can think of no better method than that of following in some detail the intellectual development of Li Ta-chao and Ch'en Tu-hsiu during the years immediately preceding the founding of the Chinese Communist Party. Not only were these men the actual founders of the Communist Party and the sponsors of Marxism-Leninism in China, but they were also among the few undisputed leaders of the whole westernized intelligentsia. Their relationship to their students at Peking University—the students of the May Fourth Movement—can hardly be understood in terms of the occidental student-professor relationship. It was much closer in spirit to the traditional Chinese sage-disciple relationship. It is, therefore, no exaggeration to say that in their reactions to the events of their day, they epitomized, to some extent, the experience of a whole segment of the advanced intelligentsia.

Ch'en Tu-hsiu,[1] the founder of the *Hsin Ch'ing-nien* review, had in the years preceding 1919 committed himself to a fairly consistent philosophy resting on the twin pillars of "democracy and science." On its negative side, this philosophy had involved a total rejection of

Excerpted by permission of the publishers from pp. 8–9, 10, 12, 13–14, 21–23 of Benjamin I. Schwartz, *Chinese Communism and the Rise of Mao*, Cambridge, Mass.: Harvard University Press, Copyright 1951 by the President and Fellows of Harvard College.

*Benjamin I. Schwartz is Professor of History and Government, Harvard University. His other publications include *In Search of Wealth and Power: Yen Fu and the West* (Harvard East Asian Series, 16, 1964).

traditional Chinese culture in all its manifestations—Buddhist, Taoist, and Confucian. Buddhism and Taoism by their radically antiworldly bias had paralyzed the energies of China for centuries. Confucianism on its side had suffocated the individual in a network of family and social obligations.[2] The final result had been passivity, stagnation, and impotence in the face of the challenge from the West. The answer to this challenge could be found only in the West itself. How was one to account for the bursting vitality of the West, its spiritual and physical dynamism? What did the West have that the East lacks? The answer in Ch'en's view was quite clear—democracy and science. It is perhaps worth noting here that, as a rebel against Chinese tradition, as a fervent "modernist," Ch'en was little inclined to seek the secret of the West in anything preceding the eighteenth century. In this he accurately mirrored the mentality of the whole advanced intelligentsia. . . .

Li Ta-chao[3] was a man of fundamentally different temper. While Ch'en Tu-hsiu concerned himself by predilection with concrete social and literary problems, Li Ta-chao was eminently a man of metaphysical bent. During his years as professor of history at Peking, he had evolved a vague and yet significant "system" which seems a strange amalgam of Chinese and Western elements. One can find here echoes of Buddha and Ch'ü Yüan, [4] of Emerson and Hegel. The outlines of this system are to be found in two essays entitled "Youth" *(Ch'ing-ch'un)*[5] and "Now" *(Chin),*[6] written at different times and yet illustrating the same fundamental theme.

•   •   •

In spite of the metaphysical cast of Li's mind, however, we soon find that, like Ch'en Tu-hsiu, he was moved by a more immediate preoccupation than the search for philosophic truth—namely, the plight of China. Essentially, Li's whole philosophy was his defiant reply to the charge that China was a dead civilization with no further possibilities of development. The Chinese nation, like mankind in general, could slough off the incubus of the past and experience a new youth in the present. "Our nation has gone through an extremely long history and the accumulated dust of the past is heavily weighing it down. By fettering its life it has brought our nation to a state of extreme decay. . . . What we must prove to the world is not that the old China is not dead, but that a new youthful China is in the process of being born."[7]

How was this rebirth to be brought about? On this point Li was vague. He did not commit himself to a whole social program as did Ch'en. He did not look to the individual or to specific socio-economic programs to bring about the rebirth, but to the historic process itself. China, in his view, was now part of the world historic process and all the upheavals and wars which distinguish the modern world must certainly be the birth pangs of a tremendous global rebirth, in which China must participate. Thus, instead of committing himself to specific solutions, he looked to the future with an air of eager anticipation.

Comparing Ch'en Tu-hsiu and Li Ta-chao at this point, we find that they were at one in their uncompromising hostility to traditional Chinese culture; that they both looked to the West for philosophic guidance and accepted this guidance uncritically. Yet, while Ch'en Tu-hsiu found in democracy and science specific solutions for China's problems—social, political, and cultural—Li Ta-chao's thought remained on the cosmic level, looking forward to some cosmic act of liberation. We are not surprised that he was the first to accept the messianic message of the October Revolution.

In Li's article entitled "The Victory of Bolshevism,"[8] written in October 1918, we already find him seizing upon the October Revolution as the very act of cosmic liberation which he had been awaiting. "The real victory," he explains, "is not the victory of the Allies against the Germans, but the victory of the Bolsheviks. . . . Henceforth all national boundaries, all differences of classes, all barriers to freedom will be swept away."[9] The eternally youthful spirit of the universe had shaken off by this one act the dusty accumulations of the past. Using his favorite image of spring and autumn, he exclaims, "The Russian Revolution has shaken off the last dismal autumn leaves from the tree of the world . . . although the word Bolshevism was created by the Russians, its spirit expresses the common sentiments of twentieth-century mankind. Thus, the victory of Bolshevism is the victory of the spirit of all mankind."[10]

It is interesting to note, however, that while Li Ta-chao had already accepted the messianic claims of the Russian revolution, he was still not a Marxist in any strict sense of the word. This very article entitled "The Victory of Bolshevism" states that "the history of Mankind is a record of its common spiritual experience. A change in the sentiments of the individual is a reflection in miniature of a change in world sentiments."[11] In other words, he still conceived of the historic process as a movement of the world spirit. He had still not "turned Hegel right side up." In Marxist terms he was still an "idealist." He hardly seemed to realize at this point that the acceptance of the Bolshevik message involved the acceptance of its dogmatic base. . . .

Unlike the leaders of social democracy in the West, Lenin had begun to occupy himself with the problem of the "backward areas" at a relatively early date. As a man who thought, above all, in terms of political action it had occurred to him that the nascent nationalism of the world's "backward areas" could itself be utilized as a force in realizing the world revolution. Thus in February 1916 he writes in *Sozialdemokrat:* "Not only would we carry out our whole minimum program with decisive means, but we would at once systematically start to incite rebellion among the peoples now oppressed by the Great Russians—and all the colonies and dependent countries of Asia (India, China, Persia, etc.)."[12] This policy was, of course, to find its theoretical framework in the famous Leninist theory of imperialism. The Leninist theory of imperialism confronted the Chinese intelligentsia with a grandiose, starkly melodramatic image of the world. Within this theory almost the entire onus for the wretchedness of the backward areas is laid at the door of international finance capital.[13] In 1919, the picture in its crude outlines seemed simple enough. On the one side was the concert of capitalist-imperialist powers—on the other, the Soviet State of Workers and Peasants, which represented the interest of the toilers as well as of all the oppressed nations and colonies. In 1919 it was an image which seemed to reflect most accurately the events of the time. Had not the Allies acted in concert at Versailles in support of Japanese imperialism? Had not the Soviet Union placed itself squarely on the side of China in its Karakhan proposal?[14]

Li Ta-chao had been won by this melodramatic vision even before the events of 1919, conceiving of it in terms of the conflict between the dead spirit of the past and mankind's self-renewal. After the events of 1919, Ch'en also began to feel its magnetic pull.

In his lectures at Peking University, Professor Dewey had made clear his rejection of all-embracing solutions for mankind's political and economic difficulties. He had viewed human experience as a sea of separate problems and had specifically stated that the only scientific approach to human problems was "to search for concrete methods to meet concrete problems according to the exigencies of time and place." Yet, it was precisely such all embracing solutions which Ch'en Tu-hsiu had sought in the West. He had hoped that "democracy and science" would have the potency of western technology, while the implementation of the democratic program he had himself outlined in his "Basis for the Realization of Democracy" would, on the contrary, have demanded long years of prosaic and undramatic work. It would have required a "going to the people" on the part of the intelligentsia with the aim of carrying on the political education of the people and of helping them to organize themselves along democratic lines. This would, in turn, have required a spirit of utter self-effacement on the part of the intelligentsia, a willingness to play a modest role in the background with no hope of immediate spectacular results. It was a role which neither Ch'en nor his students were ready to play, and a role for which traditional Chinese civilization provided few precedents. Leninism, it is true, would also require a "going to the people" and would in the next few years lead many young students to sacrifice life and career. However, the role it offered to the intelligentsia was a spectacular role of leadership in an atmosphere supercharged with the promise of imminent redemption. It called upon the intelligentsia to agitate and to organize and then to lead the organizations thus formed. It was a type of "going to the people" which Sun Yat-sen was later to find compatible with his own elitist convictions. The fact that Ch'en clearly understood the implications of Leninism on this point is indicated by a statement made in December 1920 to the effect that "a political revolution must begin with those who have knowledge, with the urban intelligentsia, while the social revolution must begin from the organized producers—the laborers."[15] It need hardly be added that like Lenin, he felt that the social revolution must be led by the political revolution.

The very issue of the *Hsin Ch'ing-nien* which carried Ch'en's article on "The Basis for the Realization of Democracy" also carried the first symptoms of his transformation. In one of his miscellaneous notes on current events, Ch'en exclaims: "They accuse the Bolsheviks of disturbing the peace. Do not the Great Powers disturb the peace when they violate the sovereignty of small and weak countries? It is the anti-Bolshevik Omsk government which has bombarded our gunboats and protested against Mongolian autonomy in the name of the Sino-Russian Treaty. It is these gentlemen who are disturbing the peace!"[16] The emotional impact of the Leninist world image was soon to efface every trace of Dewey's influence.

By September 1920, Ch'en Tu-hsiu had accepted Marxism-Leninism *in toto*. None of the philosophic hesitations which mark Li Ta-chao's approach to Marxist doctrine stood in the way of his final leap. "Democracy and Science" had failed; Professor Dewey's program would require years of undramatic self-effacing work for its implementation, and even then offered no hopes of any overall redemption. Here, at last, was a view of life marked by drastic, melodramatic contrasts and hopes of total redemption. What was more, the drama it envisaged was a global drama which finally brought China onto the stage of world history.

The same events and the same atmosphere which carried Ch'en Tu-hsiu into the Marxist-Leninist fold also served to overcome the last scruples of Li Ta-chao on the matter of Marxism. In an article entitled "Material Change and Ethical Change" published in the *Hsin Ch'ao* review in December 1919,[17] we still find, however, evidence of mental conflict. In this article Li Ta-chao tries to reconcile his fervent faith in the power of the human conscience with Marxist doctrine. He reiterates his belief that "the existence of a moral sense is something we must all accept," and that "the call of duty exists in the human heart."[18] However, the source of this moral sense need not be traced to any supernatural source, but can be found in the social instinct which the human race has developed in the course of its struggle for social existence. He thus explains the origin of the moral sense by his own peculiar version of Social Darwinism (a version in violent conflict with Thomas Henry Huxley's, as well as with other versions of European Social Darwinism).

While the moral sense itself can be explained in terms of "Darwinism," however, the positive content of various ethical systems is to be explained only in terms of changes in the mode of production. Man may indeed act out of a sense of duty, but his concept of where his duty lies is determined by the economic system in which he lives.

It is in this manner that Li finally comes to terms with Marx.

NOTES

1. See Benjamin Schwartz, "Biographical Sketch, Ch'en Tu-hsiu, Pre-Communist Phase," *Papers on China* (Harvard University, 1948), 11, 168.

2. See *ibid.*, p. 193, n. 5.

3. Born in Hopei Province in 1888, he studied political economy at the Peiyang School of Legal Administration. He later studied at Wasada University in Japan, specializing in political economy. Upon his return to China he became librarian at the Peking University library. (In 1918 Mao Tse-tung was one of his library employees.) In 1920 he became Professor of History at Peking University. During these years he helped Ch'en Tu-hsiu and Hu-Shih to edit the *Hsin ch'ing-nien*, and also helped the student body to edit the *Hsin ch'ao* (Renaissance) review. In the late months of 1920 he collaborated with Ch'en Tu-hsiu in founding the Chinese Communist Party and was later considered the virtual leader of the Communist Party in the northern provinces. In April 1927 he was arrested in the Soviet Embassy at Peking by Chang Tso-lin's troops and summarily

executed. He has been venerated ever since as one of the outstanding martyrs of the Chinese Communist movement.

4. Ch'ü Yuan. A minister of the King of Ch'ü (332–295 B.C.), he was the very prototype of the loyal minister. However, as a result of intrigues at court he was impeached and exiled. In a long elegy entitled *Li Sao*, he pours forth his disenchanted views on human destiny and the nature of the cosmos.

5. *Hsin ch'ing-nien*, vol.II, no. 1 (September 1916).

6. *Hsin ch'ing-nien*, vol. IV, no. 4 (April 1918).

7. "Ch'ing-ch'un" (Youth), *Hsin ch'ing-nien*, vol. IV, no. 4, p.6.

8. "Bolshevism ti sheng-li" (Victory of Bolshevism), *Hsin ch'ing-nien*, vol. V, no. 5 (1918). The same issue also carries an article by him entitled "Shu-min ti sheng-li" (Victory of the Masses), which is on the same theme.

9. "Bolshevism ti sheng-li," p. 443.

10. *Ibid.*, p. 447.

11. "Shu-min ti sheng-li."

12. Quoted by David Shub, *Lenin, A Biography* (New York, 1948), p.144.

13. See his *Imperialism, the Highest Stage of Capitalism* (New York, 1939).

14. It would be impossible to overestimate the impression produced in China by Karakhan's proposal. The *Hsin ch'ing-nien* issue of May 1920 (vol. VII, no. 6) carries a translation of the proposal, as well as a large collection of expressions of approval received from various organized groups throughout China; see "Tui-yü Ngo-lo-ssü Lao-nung cheng-fu t'ung-kao ti yü lun" (Expressions of Public Opinion on the Proclamation of the Russian Government of Workers and Peasants). Among the organizations represented are: "The All-China Journalists Union," "The All-China Student Federation," "Deputies of the National Assembly," "The Commercial National Salvation Association," etc. In this proclamation Karakhan states, "We shall not merely aid the workers, but also wish to aid the people of China. . . . Every nation whether large or small should have complete autonomy. We proclaim that all secret treaties made before the revolution with China, Japan, or the allies are hereby abrogated." He then specifically enumerates the treaties to be abrogated, all of which are prejudicial to Chinese sovereignty. "We hereby renounce all territory obtained through aggressive means by the former Russian imperial government in China, Manchuria, and elsewhere. . . . In short, we hereby renounce all special privileges formerly obtained by Russia in China. . . . If the Chinese people as a result of our proposals wish to become a free people and escape the evil fate of becoming a second India and Korea as has been planned for her at the Paris Peace Conference, we fervently hope that the Chinese people will make common cause with the peasants, workers, and Red soldiers of the Soviet Union and fight for their freedom!" The statements from the various organizations are replete with the most fervid expressions of gratitude and all of them, regardless of political coloration, profess to see in this act of the Soviet Union the beginning of a new era.

15. "Sui-kan-lu" (Random Thoughts), "Ko-ming yü tso-luan" (Revolution and Rebellion), *Hsin ch'ing-nien*, vol. VIII, no. 4 (December 1920), p. 3.

16. "Sui-kan-lu" (Random Thoughts), "Kuo-chi-p'ai yü shih-chieh ho-p'ing" (The Extremists and World Peace). *Hsin ch'ing-nien*, vol. VII, no. 1, pp. 115–116.

17. "Wu-chih pien-tung yü tao-te pien-tung" (Material Change and Ethical Change), *Hsin ch'ao* (Renaissance), vol. II, no. 2 (December 1919). The *Hsin ch'ao* review was a short-lived but extremely influential periodical published by a group of students at Peking University. (Its editor at the height of the May Fourth movement was Fu Ssu-nien.)

18. *Ibid.*, p. 207.

SHAO CHUAN LENG AND NORMAN D. PALMER*
Sun Yat-sen's Alliance with Russia

In 1921 the Chinese Communist Party was founded in Shanghai by Ch'en Tu-hsiu and Li Ta-chao with the active help and encouragement of Russian agents. The CCP at this stage was small and weak and hardly in a position to make an impact on the Chinese scene or significantly help further Russian diplomatic interests in China. The Russians, who had also made connections with other military and political leaders of China, felt that the greatest promise for Chinese nationalism lay with the KMT under Sun Yat-sen.

Sun Yat-sen, the veteran revolutionary leader, was now ready for an alliance with the Soviet Union. For thirty years he had worked incessantly to realize his dream of a unified Chinese Republic but had failed to get the warlord support he had sought, and had been ignored and rebuffed by the West in his appeals for help. Sun, disenchanted with the West, accepted Russian aid and was even willing to adopt Bolshevik organizational and political techniques, but he was no Communist.

The following selection describes the nature of Sun's alliance with Russia and his attitude toward the CCP.

In December 1922, Joffe arrived in Shanghai to negotiate with Dr. Sun on the question of collaboration between the Kuomintang and the Bolsheviks. After a series of discussions, they reached an agreement on the general conditions of cooperation. This agreement was announced in the form of a joint statement issued on January 26, 1923:

> 1. Dr. Sun Yat-sen holds that the Communistic order or even the Soviet system cannot actually be introduced into China, because there do not exist here the conditions for the successful establishment of either Communism or Sovietism. This view is entirely shared by Mr. Joffe, who is further of opinion that China's paramount and most pressing

From Shao Chuan Leng and Norman D. Palmer, *Sun Yat-sen and Communism* (New York: Frederick A. Praeger, Inc., 1960), pp. 62–71. Copyright, Frederick A. Praeger, Inc., 1960. Reprinted by permission.

*At the time of writing this book Shao Chuan Leng, author of *Japan and Communist China*, was Associate Professor of Foreign Affairs at the University of Virginia; Norman D. Palmer, co-author of *International Relations* and *Major Governments of Asia*, was Professor of Political Science at the University of Pennsylvania.

problem is to achieve national unification and attain full national independence, and regarding this great task he has assured Dr. Sun Yat-sen that China has the warmest sympathy of the Russian people and can count on the support of Russia.

2. In order to clarify the situation, Dr. Sun Yat-sen has requested Mr. Joffe for a reaffirmation of the principles defined in the Russian Note to the Chinese Government, dated September 27, 1920. Mr. Joffe has accordingly reaffirmed these principles and categorically declared to Dr. Sun Yat-sen that the Russian Government is ready and willing to enter into negotiation with China on the basis of the renunciation by Russia of all the treaties and exactions which the Tsardom imposed in China, including the treaty or treaties and agreement relating to the Chinese Eastern Railway. . . .

3. Recognizing that the Chinese Eastern Railway question in its entirety can be satisfactorily settled only at a competent Russo-Chinese Conference, Dr. Sun Yat-sen is of the opinion that the realities of the situation point to the desirability of a *modus vivendi* in the matter of the present management of the Railway. . . .

4. Mr. Joffe has categorically declared to Dr. Sun Yat-sen . . . that it is not and has never been the intention or purpose of the present Russian Government to pursue an imperialistic policy in Outer Mongolia or to cause it to secede from China. Dr. Sun Yat-sen, therefore, does not view an immediate evacuation of Russian troops from Outer Mongolia as imperative or in the real interest of China. . . . [1]

This joint statement received wide publicity in China, but its significance was generally overlooked abroad. Whatever secret agreements there may have been between Dr. Sun and Joffe, a careful examination of their statement itself reveals some interesting points. First, the Sun-Joffe declaration officially marked the beginning of friendly cooperation between the Kuomintang and Soviet Russia and constituted the basis for their alliance. While no formal alliance against Chinese warlords and Western imperialism was announced in this document, Russia did pledge to support the Kuomintang in its efforts to "achieve unification and attain full national independence" of China. Furthermore, it was the first time that a European power treated a Chinese regime on equal terms. Second, the declaration indicated that the alliance Sun sought with Russia was a qualified arrangement. He accepted Soviet aid, in his attempt to achieve the Chinese revolution, only after the Russians pledged not to impose Communism on China and agreed to surrender all their special positions in China. So far as the Bolsheviks were concerned, they did not try to convert Sun to Communism. For the fight against a common enemy—foreign imper-

while itself rejecting the west

alism—and for their future success in China, they were willing to make temporary concessions to win the confidence of Dr. Sun and his followers. Third, the joint statement was obviously the result of prolonged, give-and-take negotiations, as the spirit of compromise was quite in evidence. Taking the Chinese Eastern Railway question as an example, while both sides agreed that the whole issue should be settled at a future conference, Dr. Sun in the meantime had to accept "a *modus vivendi* in the matter of the present management of the Railway." On the question of Outer Mongolia, Russia recognized Chinese sovereignty and denied having any imperialist designs, and, once again, Sun accepted the realities of the situation by agreeing not to "view an immediate evacuation of Russian troops from Outer Mongolia as imperative or in the real interest of China."

Immediately following the conclusion of the Sun-Joffe agreement, Eugene Ch'en, personal secretary and right-hand man to Dr. Sun, publicly lauded the collaboration between the Kuomintang and Soviet Russia, and predicted defeat for the encircling policy of the "Anglo-Latin conquerors." According to Ch'en, the conversations with Joffe necessarily altered the international rating of Sun Yat-sen, who emerged as a world force with the support of Russia. The ultimate outcome of the policy underlying the conversations, Ch'en emphasized, depended on the attitude of the great powers toward Russia and toward Sun Yat-sen. "That outcome might be the contemplation of Russia and China in making available their resources to the uses of humanity—or a continued hostility to Russia, and what appears like hostility to Sun Yat-sen on the part of certain great powers might forge an iron alliance between China and Russia directed to other ends."[2] . . .

On January 15, 1923, a few days before Sun's joint declaration with Joffe, his supporters recovered Canton from the hands of Ch'en Ch'iung-ming. In February, Dr. Sun again returned to power in Canton. Meanwhile, one of his trusted aides, Liao Chung-k'ai, had accompanied Joffe to Japan to continue the negotiations.[3] After a month of detailed discussions with Joffe on the real situation in Russia, the Bolsheviks' policies and techniques, and the question of Kuomintang reorganization, Liao reported to Sun and helped push forward the Canton-Moscow collaboration. According to one account, in their talks Liao asked Joffe about the time needed for Communism to be realized in Russia and received the answer that it would probably take a hundred years. This prompted Liao to remark to a friend: "What is the use of dreaming about a Utopia which might or might not be realized, when we are all dead? Let us all be revolutionaries today, and work for the accomplishment of the national revolution on the basis of the Three People's Principles. These we can realize within our lifetime. We must, however, unite with all the revolutionary forces available, and agree on an immediate common aim no matter what our ultimate ideals are."[4] There is little doubt that Liao also used the same argument to lessen the fear of many Kuomintang leaders and to convince them of the necessity of cooperating with the Communists.

In August 1923, Dr. Sun sent a delegation headed by General Chiang Kai-shek, his Chief-of-Staff, to Moscow to study Soviet conditions and to negotiate for Russia's aid. Chiang carried with him identical letters of introduction from Dr. Sun to Lenin, Trotsky, and Chicherin. The following month, in reply to the greetings from Leo Karakhan, who had just arrived in Peking to replace Joffe as Soviet envoy, Dr. Sun stated that the purpose of Chiang's mission to Russia was "to discuss ways and means whereby our friends there can assist me in my work in this country. In particular, General Chiang is to take up with your government and military experts a proposal for military action by my forces in and about the regions lying to the northwest of Peking and beyond. General Chiang is fully empowered to act in my behalf."[5]

During their three months in Russia, Chiang and his group studied the military and political organizations, examined the industrial and agricultural systems, and attended mass meetings and discussion groups. Chiang met many Soviet leaders and had various talks with them. He was impressed by men like Trotsky, Zinoviev, Radek, Kamenev, Chicherin, and Joffe, who expressed regard for Dr. Sun and a sincere desire to cooperate with China in her national revolution. On the other hand, Chiang also found that the Soviet attitude toward Outer Mongolia was very evasive, and he was offended by the "shocking" resolution on the Kuomintang passed by the Comintern. Therefore, he began to entertain some doubts about the sincerity of the Russians.[6]

In the meantime, important steps had been taken by Moscow to assist Dr. Sun and his regime. The disillusion with General Wu P'ei-fu, who in February 1923 massacred many workers taking part in the Communist-organized Peking-Hankow Railway Strike, further convinced the Russians that Sun was the only influential ally they could find in China.[7] In September, Moscow dispatched Michael Borodin to Canton as political adviser to the Kuomintang. Ostensibly, he was to serve only in a private capacity, but, in actuality, he was appointed as an official representative of the Soviet government in Canton. He was to "take his orders direct from Moscow" and to have an important role in shaping up Soviet decisions and measures "regarding questions of the general policy of the Kuomintang in China."[8] An experienced organizer who had served abroad as an agent of the Third International, Mr. Borodin was highly recommended to Dr. Sun by a personal letter from Leo Karakhan:

> The absence in Canton of a permanent and responsible representative of our government has long been keenly felt at Moscow. With the appointment of M. M. Borodin, an important step has been taken in this direction. Comrade B. [sic] is one of the oldest members of our Party, having worked for a great many years in the revolutionary movement of Russia. Please regard Comrade B. not only as a representative of the government but likewise my personal representative with whom you may talk as frankly as you would with me. Anything he says, you may rely upon as if I had said it to you personally. He is familiar with the whole situation and besides, before his leaving for the South, we had a long talk. He will convey to you my thoughts, wishes, feelings.[9]

The main objectives of the Borodin mission were to use the Soviet example to help reorganize Sun's Party and Army, to formalize the relations between the Kuomintang and the Chinese Communists, and to turn the Chinese revolution into an antimilitarist, anti-imperialist mass movement. Concerned over the Kuomintang's failure to organize the masses, the Russians repeatedly told Sun of the importance of broadening the basis of his Party. In a letter to the Chinese leader on December 4, 1923, Chicherin declared: "We think that the fundamental aim of the Kuomintang Party is to build up a great, powerful movement of the Chinese people and that therefore propaganda and organization on the biggest scale are its first necessities." Citing Soviet experiences as a significant example, he explained that "our military activities were successful because a long series of years had elapsed during which we organized and instructed our followers, building up in this way a great, organized party throughout the whole land, a party capable of vanquishing all its adversaries."[10] Karakhan also wrote to Dr. Sun on January 7, 1924, to the same effect. He urged Sun to carry out land reform, to mobilize popular support, and, above all, to strengthen the Kuomintang.[11]

When Borodin arrived in Canton in October 1923, he found Sun's regime in a precarious position, constantly threatened by Ch'en Ch'iung-ming's forces. He first assured Dr. Sun that Communism was not suitable for present conditions in China, and that he would support the fight for the realization of the Three People's Principles. Then he was quick to point out certain serious shortcomings with the Kuomintang: "In the first place, the Kuomintang organization is very incomplete, and there is no discipline worth speaking of. Second, there are many impure elements in the Kuomintang, corrupt bureaucrats and adventurers. Then the Kuomintang lacks a popular basis in the form of the organization of the masses."[12] All these things had to be rectified, said the Soviet representative, before the Kuomintang could become an effective revolutionary weapon. To this suggestion, Dr. Sun agreed completely. Borodin also promised Sun to obtain arms and munitions on easy terms from Soviet Russia and to provide a corps of military and civilian experts to help Canton in the reorganization work.[13]

There is little doubt that Borodin quickly won Sun's confidence and soon became the "reorganizer" of the Kuomintang. In a speech given on November 25, 1923, Dr. Sun told his followers that the Russian Communist Party actually advocated the Three People's Principles of the Kuomintang. The reason for the success of the Russian revolution was that the Russians had good methods and organization, and that their Party members struggled for the realization of their principles. In order to learn their methods, Sun said, he had asked Mr. Borodin to undertake the task of training the Kuomintang members. "Since Mr. Borodin is extremely experienced in Party management," Sun continued, "all the comrades are expected to sacrifice their personal prejudices and to learn faithfully his methods."[14] Thus, with the backing of Sun and the help of other Russian advisers, Borodin started an unprecedented job of reorganizing the Kuomintang, and revolutionizing its army, all along Soviet lines.

THE ADMITTANCE OF THE CHINESE COMMUNISTS INTO THE KUOMINTANG

The story of the Moscow-Canton entente will not be complete if the admission of the Chinese Communists into the Kuomintang is left unexamined. It should be recalled that, under the pressure of Maring, the Chinese Communist Party in 1922 made concessions to the Kuomintang, in the search for a formula for their cooperation. Nevertheless, there was apparent reluctance on the part of the Chinese Communist leadership to seek such an alliance, and this attitude was criticized as being impractical by Karl Radek at the Fourth Congress of the Comintern, in November 1922.[15] The Executive Committee of the Communist International, in a resolution of January 12, 1923, further laid down the proper course of action for the Chinese Party. Calling the Kuomintang the only important national-revolutionary group in China, the resolution stated: "Insofar as the independent working class movement in the country is still weak, insofar as the central task confronting China is to carry out the national revolution against the imperialists and their feudal agents . . . the E.C.C.I. considers that it is necessary to coordinate the activities of the Kuomintang and of the young Communist Party of China."[16] The Party was, however, advised not to merge with the Kuomintang but to preserve its complete political and organizational independence, while working inside the latter. It was against this background of the Kremlin's pressure, together with the demoralizing failure of the Hankow strike of February 1923, that the Third National Congress of the Chinese Communist Party in June 1923 officially approved the formula of entering the Kuomintang. The Congress Manifesto described the Kuomintang as "the central force of the national revolution" and called upon "all the revolutionary elements in our society" to "rally to the Kuomintang, speeding up the completion of the national-revolutionary movement." At the same time, it made clear that "the Chinese Communist Party never forgets for one moment to support the interests of the workers and peasants. . . . Our mission is to liberate the oppressed Chinese nation by a national revolution, and to advance to the world revolution, liberating the oppressed peoples and oppressed classes of the whole world."[17]

With the Chinese Communists' formal concession of the leadership to the Kuomintang, the Moscow-Canton entente passed its final hurdle. Although certain elements in the Kuomintang were, from the beginning, opposed to the idea of admitting the Communists into the Party, Dr. Sun was able to bring them into line.[18] In January 1924, Sun's policy of alliance with Soviet Russia and of admitting the Communists into the Kuomintang received official endorsement from the First National Congress of the Kuomintang, held in Canton. In presenting his new policy, Sun told the Congress of its necessity for the Chinese revolution, and of the good intentions of Soviet Russia in helping the Kuomintang. Concerning the admittance of the Chinese Communists into the Party, he pointed out: "The Communists are joining our Party in order to work for the national revolution. We are, therefore, bound to admit them. If our own members are only active in their propaganda of the principles of the Party, and build up a strong organization and submit unquestioningly to Party discipline, we need have nothing to fear from Communist machinations. In any case, if the Communists betray the Kuomintang, I will be the first to propose their expulsion."[19] In spite of Sun's explanation, some members were still not satisfied. They proposed a strict Party regulation that "a Kuomintang member should not join the other Party," as a means to restrict the Communists. Li Ta-chao, a Communist delegate, then assured the Congress with the following statement: "We join this Party as individuals, not as a body. We may be said to have dual Party membership. But it may not be said of Kuomintang that there is a Party within a Party. . . . Since we have joined the Party and so long as we remain its members, we shall carry out its political program and abide by its constitution and bylaws. We shall obey the disciplinary measures or punishment imposed by this Party in case we fail to do so."[20] This statement was accepted by the Congress, and admission of the Communists became an official Kuomintang policy. A few Communists even became members of the Central Executive Committee of the Kuomintang.[21]

NOTES

1. *The China Year Book, 1928* (Tientsin: The Tientsin Press, 1928), p. 1318.

2. *The New York Times*, January 28, 1923.

3. Liao, one of the leaders of the Kuomintang's Left Wing, was assassinated on Auguse 20, 1925.

4. T'ang Leang-li, *The Inner History of the Chinese Revolution* (New York: E. P. Dutton & Co., 1930), p. 158.

5. Typed copy of original file of Sun-Karakhan correspondence in the personal collection of Louis Fischer, quoted in Allen Whiting, *Soviet Policies in China, 1917–1924* (New York: Columbia University Press, 1954), p. 243.

6. For Chiang's account of his trip to Russia, see Chiang Kai-shek, *Soviet Russia in China* (New York: Farrar, Straus and Cudahy, 1957), pp. 19–25; Shih-i Hsiung, *The Life of Chiang Kai-shek* (London: P. Davies, 1948), pp. 175–179.

7. Wu and Sun were previously considered potential allies by Moscow. The feeling of bitterness after the incident was recorded by Pavel Mif: "The shooting down of the workers dispersed all illusions concerning Wu Pei-fu, whom hitherto a number of workers' organizations regarded as a 'friend of the workers' and as 'being in favor of working-class legislation.' It became clear to every worker that Wu Pei-fu was a servant of the foreign capitalist." *Heroic China* (New York: Workers' Library Publishers, 1937), p. 20.

8. See the extract from a telegram, dated November 12, 1926, sent by the Commissariat of Foreign Affairs at Moscow to the Soviet representative at Peking, as disclosed in a *White Paper* issued by the British Foreign Office on May 26, 1927, following the raid on Arcos House. *The China Year Book, 1928*, pp. 823–824.

9. This was the letter Karakhan wrote to Sun on September 23, 1923. For the text, see Whiting, *op. cit.*, p. 244.

10. Louis Fischer, *The Soviets in World Affairs* (London: Jonathan Cape, 1930), Vol. II, p. 635.

11. *Ibid.*, pp. 635–636.

12. T'ang Leang-li, *op. cit.*, p. 160.

13. *The China Year Book, 1928*, p. 1321.

14. *Tsung-li ch'üan-shu* [*Complete Writings of President Sun*], (Taipeh: The China Culture Service, 1953), Vol. 7, part II, p. 752.

15. Radek warned: "You must understand, comrades, that neither the question of socialism nor of the Soviet republic are now the order of the day. . . . The immediate task is: (1) To organize the young working class. (2) To regulate its relations with the revolutionary bourgeoisie elements in order to organize the struggle against the European and Asiatic imperialism." Benjamin Schwartz, *Chinese Communism and the Rise of Mao* (Cambridge: Harvard University Press, 1951), p. 37.

16. Mif, *op. cit.*, pp. 21–22.

17. For the full text of the manifesto, see Conrad Brandt, Benjamin Schwartz, and John K. Fairbank, *A Documentary History of Chinese Communism* (Cambridge: Harvard University Press, 1952), pp. 71–72. It should be noted that interesting criticism of the Kuomintang's past mistakes was also voiced by the Manifesto, which demanded that "the Kuomintang will resolutely discard its two old notions of reliance on foreign powers and concentration on military action, and that it will pay attention to political propaganda among the people."

18. C. Martin Wilbur and Julie L. Y. How (eds.), *Documents on Communism, Nationalism, and Soviet Advisers in China* (New York: Columbia University Press, 1956), pp. 148–149.

19. T'ang Leang-li, *op. cit.*, p. 178.

20. Chiang Kai-shek, *op. cit.*, p. 27.

21. Of the twenty-four Committee members, three were Communists, including Li Ta-chao and T'an P'ing-shan. Of the seventeen Reserve CEC members, six were Communists, including Chang Kuo-t'ao, Ch'ü Ch'iu-pai, and Mao Tse-tung. Probably more important, T'an P'ing-shan became the head of the Department of Organization of the Kuomintang.

CH'IEN TUAN-SHENG*

Sun Yat-Sen's Reorganized Ideas

Sun Yat-sen took Russian advice in reorganizing his party and Russian aid in building up a party army, while making it quite clear that he had no liking for Communism. He reiterated his faith in his own formula for the Chinese Revolution. It is, however, worthy of note that the Three People's Principles, as stated in the January

Reprinted by permission of the publishers from Ch'ien Tuan-sheng, *The Government and Politics of China*, pp. 112–115. Cambridge, Mass.: Harvard University Press, Copyright 1950 by the President and Fellows of Harvard College.

*Ch'ien Tuan-sheng took his doctorate in Government from Harvard University in the 1920s and was later a leading professor of political science at major universities in China.

1924 Manifesto of the First Kuomintang Congress, had undergone discernible changes.

Sun Yat'sen's Three Principles of the People are the Principles of *Min-tsu, Min-ch'üan*, and *Min-sheng,* or, respectively, People's Nationhood, People's Power, and People's Livelihood. The first two can certainly be rendered as ''Nationalism'' and ''Democracy,'' for they are not different from them. The Principle of the People's Livelihood is neither socialism nor communism, and to translate it as ''Socialism'' would be out of place. It is better to let either *Min-sheng* or People's Livelihood stand.

1. Nationalism The nationalist concept of Sun Yat-sen went through three successive phases. The first phase was simple. The Manchus who had ruled over China were considered an alien race denying self-government to the Chinese. Chinese nationalism demanded the liquidation of that group. When the Manchus were gone, the Chinese Republic of 1912 was regarded as a political community in which the five races, the Chinese, the Manchus, the Mongols, the Mohammedans, and the Tibetans, formed one inseparable unit. Nobody cared to subject that vague and confused conception to historical and ethnological analysis. Sun Yat-sen himself was no exception. For years he said almost nothing about his first Principle. In the 1914 statute of his newly christened Chinese Revolutionary Party, it was formally provided that the aims of the party were to fulfill the Principles of People's Power and People's Livelihood. At that time Sun Yat-sen must have felt that his first Principle had been fully realized.

A new interpretation of nationalism began with Sun Yat-sen's own disillusionment with the Powers and with the rise of the student movement and his contact with Soviet ideas. By 1924 the Principle had acquired new meaning and new substance. Nationalism is anti-imperialistic in its external aspect, and embraces self-determination of the racial minorities within the borders of China. It can be realized only by a nationalist revolution against imperialist control and also against the Chinese elements which have conspired with or tolerated the imperialists. Further, the Chinese were also to help other oppressed nations, especially those in the East, to shake off their foreign yokes. It is therefore also to be a world revolution of the oppressed nations. In this, Sun Yat-sen's nationalism differed little, if any, from the Soviet tenets at the time.

But in two aspects Sun Yat-sen was uniquely Chinese. First, he was in favor of self-determination for the minorities in China, or, in the words of the Manifesto, the "several nationalities" of China were to enjoy the rights of self-determination and finally to federate themselves into a Chinese republic. Yet at the same time he also said that national assimilation does not run counter to the Principle of Nationalism. Here he seemed to be saying that if the Chinese had succeeded in assimilating other races, the latter need not seek self-determination. Second, Sun Yat-sen continued to cherish the Confucianist idea of a "Great Commonwealth" which would comprise all mankind and would naturally obliterate all national and racial demarcations.

2. Democracy   Sun Yat-sen's second Principle also experienced historical changes and graftings. With one exception, there was nothing to show that Sun Yat-sen's earlier concept of the Principle was anything other than the kind of democracy which prevailed in the contemporary West. The exception was that Sun Yat-sen did from very early times advocate a period of tutelage. His party was to enjoy exclusive political power during the period, and the veteran members were even to enjoy political privileges during their lifetime. But this was not to be a thing of permanence; it did not really cut into the principle of democracy.

With the coming of the Soviet anti-parliamentarian doctrine, coupled with the revulsion which the failures of the Chinese Parliament had created in him, he began to be harshly critical of the representative democracies of the West, considering them to be both anti-nationalist and anti-Min-sheng. Anti-nationalist because the Western democracies allowed only self-rule for the dominant race, leaving other nations or races subjected and oppressed. Anti-Min-sheng because the capitalists of the Western democracies denied livelihood to the less fortunate classes.

According to Sun Yat-sen, therefore, a tenable Principle of People's Power, or real democracy, must be in full conformity with the other two Principles. He proposed that the people should exercise directly the four powers of election, recall, initiative, and referendum. With these four powers directly exercised by the people, there would be no danger of the people ever losing their power over government. Then he went on to put what he terms "powers and functions" in juxtaposition. While the people should have the full enjoyment of powers, the functions should nevertheless be vested in the unfettered hands of the government equally fully. There were to be five functions, namely, executive, legislative, judicial, control, and examination. With gusto he argued for the separation of the functions of control and examination from the three older powers defined by Montesquieu.

Thus Sun Yat-sen advocated a government capable of the full exercise of five functions or, as he calls it, "an all-function government." At the same time he cast aspersions on the idea of natural rights. In subsequent years this has given rise to a school of interpretation which has done yeoman service to justify the disregard, if not suppression, of popular freedoms, and the emergence of an irresponsible and dictatorial, if not also totalitarian, government. A more sensible interpretation of Sun Yat-sen's second Principle would have emphasized the more positive aspect of his concept of the People's Political Powers, rather than either his criticism of representative democracy or his partisanship for a strong government. In the whole scheme of his second Principle, strong government certainly occupies only an auxiliary place, whereas the enjoyment of full political powers by the people was his main concern.

3. *Min-sheng*   The Livelihood Principle is not so susceptible to fair and intelligent interpretation. That Principle presents both a theory and a number of proposals. Sun Yat-sen was opposed to Karl Marx's materialist interpretation of history. He had no sympathy for the class struggle of Marx. Nor did he accept the Marxian theory of surplus value. He did not quite say that he would oppose his own interpretation of history to the materialism of Marx, but if any of his followers should, as some now do, pit Min-sheng-ism against materialism, or the Min-sheng interpretation of history against the materialist interpretation of history, they certainly cannot be accused of fabrication. Indeed, in his acceptance of an obscure American author's "social interpretation of history"[1] Sun Yat-sen accepted the idea that "livelihood is the central force in social progress, and that social progress is the central force in history; hence the struggle for a living and not material forces determines history."[2] Thinking along this social line, Sun Yat-sen, though recognizing the existence of classes, also repudiated class struggle, and favored conciliation among classes.

As for more concrete proposals, Sun Yat-sen advocated the equalization of land tenure, and the regulation of capital. To achieve the former, he proposed that the unearned increment of land value should accrue to the state. To achieve the latter, he proposed state ownership of principal industries and enterprises. While lack of precision characterizes the latter proposal, a lack of comprehensiveness marks the former. Finally his famous answer to the question, "What is the Principle of Livelihood?"—"It is communism and it is socialism,"confounds his readers still further.

In justice to Sun Yat-sen it must be said that his economic thinking was progressive and that he was genuinely interested in the welfare of the little man. But he never formulated a well-thought-out economic theory or a well-planned economic program.

It is then not unfair to observe that the chief innovation in the revised Three Principles of 1924 was the harnessing of anti-imperialist sentiment, which was then popular with the more forwarding-looking elements of the country, to give the party a new battle cry and to accelerate the downfall of its enemies. The other aspects of the Principles were of no urgent import at the moment and they were still vague and obscure.[3]

NOTES

1. Maurice William, *The Social Interpretation of History* (1921). See also his *Sun Yat-sen versus Communism* (1932).

2. *San Min Chu I,* translated into English by Frank W. Price, edited by L. T. Chen (Shanghai: Institute of Pacific Affairs, 1927), p. 383.

3. See Tsui Shu-chin, "The Influence of the Canton-Moscow Entente upon Sun Yat-sen's Political Philosophy and Revolutionary Tactics" (MS, 1933).

IV For Whom the Revolution?

In earlier sections we have seen how a massive intellectual revolution was under way within China and how a spirit of patriotism and nationalism was creating pressures for further change. It must be remembered, however, that this impressive intellectual ferment was taking place only within urban communities and, as yet, hardly touched the vast countryside. The peasantry, which formed the bulk of China's population, still led an impoverished existence within the framework of traditional beliefs and repressive institutions. For the revolution to succeed, "new ideas" had to provide a solution to the endemic problems of hunger and disease which affected millions of lives and "new culture" had to reach out to transform rural society.

The political parties that developed after the May Fourth Movement did not fully realize that poor peasants, if organized and given a sense of purpose and direction, could provide an inexhaustible source of revolutionary strength. It was left to Mao Tse-tung to make this discovery.

In the selections below, our intention is not to give an analysis of rural class structure, the scale of land rents and land taxes, or the exploitative role of landlords and moneylenders, but a picture of conditions in the countryside that emerged as an end result.

R. H. TAWNEY*
Poverty, War, and Famine

Writing in 1931 about the Chinese peasantry, Tawney's conclusion is: "The revolution of 1911 was a bourgeois affair. The revolution of the peasants has still to come. If their rulers continue to exploit them, or to permit them to be exploited, as remorselessly as hitherto, it is likely to be unpleasant. It will not, perhaps, be undeserved."

No comprehensive evidence exists as to the pecuniary income of Chinese farmers, and the scraps of evidence available can be briefly summarised. The most extensive survey was that made by the International Famine Relief Commission in 1922, which covered two hundred and forty villages, with 7,079 families containing 37,191 members, in the five provinces of Hopei, Kiangsu, Shantung, Anhwei and Cheki-ang.[1] It found that 17.6 per cent of the families in the eastern villages, and 62.2 per cent of those in the northern, had incomes of less than $50 a year. An inquiry made by Mr. Lee and Mr. Chin into two villages in the neighbourhood of Peiping showed that, in one of them, thirty-four out of one hundred families had incomes of less than $100, and thirty-nine of over $100 but less than $200, while, in the other, fifteen out of sixty-four families had less than $100 and eighteen more than $100 but less than $200.[2] The investigations of Professor Buck into the conditions prevailing among farmers in nine villages in north, and eight in east-central, China, yield somewhat similar results. In the former, the median income of the families studied was $131.08; in two out of the nine villages it was less than $100, and in three over $100 but less than $150. In the latter, the median income was $213.6; in one village it was under $200, and in three over $200 but less than $250. The average

---

Reprinted with the permission of Farrar, Straus & Giroux, Inc. from *Land and Labor in China* by R. H. Tawney, originally published 1932 by George Allen & Unwin Ltd., reprinted in 1964 by Octagon Books, pp. 69–77. Reprinted by permission of George Allen & Unwin also.

*R. H. Tawney (1880–1962), English economic historian and social critic of his day, taught at Oxford and the London School of Economics. Many of his books like *The Acquisitive Society* (1921) and *Religion and the Rise of Capitalism* became classics. *Land and Labor in China* was the result of his contribution to the Conference of the Institute of Pacific Relations held at Shanghai in 1931.

income per individual in the first group was $36.22, and in the second $68.17.[3]

More than one attempt has been made to estimate the minimum income needed to support a family in China. Professor Dittmer, on the basis of an investigation into the budgets of two hundred families in the neighbourhood of Peiping, put it in1918 at $100. Professor Tayler, who supervised the inquiry made by the International Famine Relief Commission, put it at $150, an estimate which is accepted by Mr. Mallory.[4] If the latter figure be adopted, more than half the families in the eastern villages then examined, and more than four-fifths in the northern, had an income below the minimum required to support life. In five out of the seventeen villages studied by Professor Buck, the median income fell below the same figure.

Evidence so limited, though the best obtainable, does not, it is obvious, carry one far. On the other hand, it is known that the minute size of holdings, which is one fundamental cause of low agricultural incomes, is a phenomenon found in all parts of China, except the three north-eastern provinces. Mere acreage, it is true, is not the only point to be considered. Types of climate and soil, methods of cultivation, and social habits are also important. The rural population of Japan, where farms are no larger than in China, has a higher standard of life; and the quality of farming in China, both in its technique and business organisation, is capable of improvement. But the small area of land at the disposal of more than half the peasants in China is undoubtedly, in itself, a cruel disability. Dr. Lieu and Dr. Chung Min-chen[5] have calculated that, in China as a whole, three mow of land (0.45 acres) per person, or 2.25 acres per family of five individuals, is required to supply the bare requirements of food alone, irrespective of housing, farm equipment, clothing, fuel and other necessities. The figures published by the Department of Agriculture and Commerce in 1917 showed that 36 per cent of the farms in China were under ten mow (1.5 acres) and another 26 per cent from ten to twenty-nine mow (4.3 acres). If they may be accepted, as in view of other evidence seems probable, as approximately correct, between 40 and 50 per cent of the peasant families in China have land insufficient, on the estimate of Dr. Lieu and Dr. Chung Min-chen, to provide them with food, apart from all their other requirements. The very high percentage which food absorbs of the family expenditure, the almost complete absence of meat from the diet of most agricultural families, the low standards of housing, the fact that the size of the family is plainly limited by the size of the holding and declines with the decline of the latter, the prevalence of ill-health, and the high rate both of general and infantile mortality in such districts as have been investigated, point in the same direction. There is even some reason to believe that, with the increased pressure on the land caused by the growth of population, the condition of the rural population, in some parts of China, may be actually worse than it was two centuries ago.[6]

Exaggeration is easy. Privation is one thing, poverty to the point of wretchedness—*la misère*—another. A sturdy and self-reliant stock may grow in a stony soil. But, when due allowance has been made for the inevitable misconceptions, it is difficult to resist the conclusion that a large proportion of Chinese peasants are constantly on the brink of actual destitution. They are, so to say, a propertied proletariat, which is saved—when it is saved—partly by its own admirable ingenuity and fortitude, partly by the communism of the Chinese family, partly by reducing its consumption of necessaries and thus using up its physical capital. "The small incomes," to quote the most distinguished foreign authority on Chinese agriculture, "reduce most of the farmers and their families to a mere subsistence basis. In fact the people feed themselves in winter, just as one 'roughs' labour animals through the winter, by consuming as little and as poor food as possible."[7]

A population which has no reserves is helpless against calamity. Calamity is more frequent in China than in the West, even when allowance is made for the different form which it assumes in the latter. It is occasioned partly by civil disorder. Here again, it is necessary to avoid exaggeration. An English Chief Justice once described the special failing of his fellow-countrymen as robbery under arms. The slaughter of combatants in China is not comparable to that of the years 1914–1918 in Europe. The miseries inflicted on the civil population, though shocking, are probably less atrocious than those which accompanied the Thirty Years' War.

It is true, however, that, over a large area of China, the rural population suffers horribly through the insecurity of life and property. It is taxed by one ruffian who calls himself a general, by another, by a third, and, when it has bought them off, still owes taxes to the Government; in some places actually more than twenty years' taxation has been paid in advance. It is squeezed by dishonest officials. It must cut its crops at the point of the bayonet, and hand them over without payment to the local garrison, though it will starve without them. It is forced to grow opium in defiance of the law, because its military tyrants can squeeze heavier taxation from opium than from rice or wheat, and make money, in addition, out of the dens where it is smoked. It pays blackmail to the professional bandits in its neighbourhood; or it resists, and, a year later, when the bandits have assumed uniform, sees its villages burned to the ground.

There is a case, no doubt, for the bandit, though it is seldom stated. He is often a disbanded soldier who, as in the England of More, is driven "either to starve or manfully to play the thief," or a victim of oppression who robs his robbers. Unfortunately, it is easier to shear sheep than wolves, and, though popular sympathy is sometimes with him, the majority of his victims are worse off than himself. It is not surprising that, in certain provinces, the peasants have armed and formed leagues to keep out "bandits, communists and government soldiers." Much that the press ascribes to communist machinations seems, indeed, to the western observer to have as much, or as little, connection with theoretical communism as the Peasants' Revolt of 1381 in England or the *Jacquerie* in France. What is called the communist question is in reality, in most parts of the country, either a land question or a question of banditry provoked by lack of employment. It appears to be true, nevertheless, that in China, as elsewhere, an elemental revolt against intolerable injustices has been organised and given a doctrinal edge by political missionaries, and that certain regions, such as parts of Fukien, Kiangsi and Hunan—the last two areas with an abnormally high percentage of tenants, and acute agrarian discontent—form *enclaves* of revolution, where such government as exists is conducted by communists. The revolution of 1911 was a bourgeois affair. The revolution of the peasants has still to come. If their rulers continue to exploit them, or to permit them to be exploited, as remorselessly as hitherto, it is likely to be unpleasant. It will not, perhaps, be undeserved.

The indirect effects of the chaos are as disastrous as the direct. Expenditure on war absorbs resources which should be spent on elementary improvements, such as roads and primary education. Trade is paralysed, and such communications as exist are turned by the soldiers who seize them from a blessing into a curse. Capital flies from rural districts, where it is urgently needed, to be buried in the Concessions. Population flies with it; here and there whole villages are on the move, like animals breaking from cover as the beaters advance. When human enemies are absent, the farmer must still reckon with a remorseless nature. "What drove you to settle here, so far from home?" a peasant was asked in the presence of the writer. The reply was, "Bandits, soldiers and famine."[8]

Famine is the feature of Chinese economic life of which the West hears most. It is an evil so appalling that all other issues seem, at first sight, trivial. The facts have been described by skilled observers, and it is needless to labour them. Such historical evidence as is available shows that distress caused by flood and drought, on a scale sufficiently large to attract public attention, has been a recurrent feature of Chinese history. As long ago as 1878, statistics compiled by Sir Alexander Hosie[9] from Chinese records showed that, in the thousand years between 620 and 1619, drought was reported in one part of the country or another at intervals of eight to twelve years—the provinces most frequently affected by it being those of the north and centre. Mr. Ta Chen[10] has published similar figures for the sixteenth and seventeenth centuries, and has shown that emigration has been related to the occurrence of exceptional distress in China. Dr. Co-ching Chu[11] has continued the record down to the present century. His figures show that, in the two hundred and fifty-six years between 1644 and 1900, there were three provinces in which flood occurred more than once in every three years, three in which it occurred more than once in every four, and three in which it occurred more than once in every five. Reports of drought were somewhat less frequent. It is stated to have occurred in one province at intervals of less than four years, in two at intervals of less than seven, and in two at intervals of less than nine. The four provinces which were the principal victims of floods, namely Chihli (now Hopei), Shantung, Kiangsu and Anhwei, were also those which suffered most severely from drought. If the figures could be trusted, they would indicate that floods were somewhat, and droughts considerably, more frequent in the two and a half centuries from 1644 to 1900 than in those preceding them. But the evidence as to the later is fuller, no doubt, than for the earlier period. All that can be reasonably inferred from it is that there has been no visible improvement.

The number of deaths caused by famine has been variously estimated. That of 1849 is said to have destroyed 13,750,000 persons; the Taiping Rebellion, with the widespread economic ruin which accompanied it, 20,000,000; the famine of 1878–79, 9,000,000 to 13,000,000; that of 1920–21, 500,000. In reality, however, to concentrate attention on these sensational catastrophes, as though life ran smoothly in the intervals between them, is to misconceive the situation. Famine is a matter of degree; its ravages are grave long before its symptoms become sufficiently shocking to arouse general consternation. If the meaning of the word is a shortage of food on a scale sufficient to cause widespread starvation, then there are parts of the country from which famine is rarely absent. In Shensi, stated an eminent Chinese official at the beginning of 1931, 3,000,000 persons had died of hunger in the last few years, and the misery had been such that 400,000 women and children had changed hands by sale. In Kansu, according to Mr. Findlay Andrew, one-third of the population has died since 1926, owing to famine, civil war, banditry and typhus.[12] There are districts in which the position of the rural population is that of a man standing permanently up to the neck in water, so that even a ripple is sufficient to drown him. The loss of life caused by the major disasters is less significant than the light which they throw on the conditions prevailing even in normal times over considerable regions.

In the case of famine, in short, as in that of war, the occasion of the breakdown must be distinguished from its causes. The former is commonly a failure of crops caused by drought or flood. The latter, though aggravated at present by political anarchy, consist in the primitive organisation, and absence of surplus resources over daily needs, which turn the misfortune of individuals into a general catastrophe.[13] It is probable that drought, if not flood, is in some measure unavoidable; there are regions in the north-west where, there is reason to believe, the desert may be advancing and progressive desiccation taking place. But one reason, at least, for the occurrence of both on a scale sufficient to produce disaster is that nature has not been subjected to control to the extent which, given a settled economic policy, and the means to carry it out, is to-day practicable. Those directly affected by them cannot meet the blow, for they have no reserves. The individual cannot be rescued by his neighbours, since whole districts together are in the same position. The district cannot be rescued by the nation, because means of communication do not permit of food being moved in sufficient quantities. Famine is, in short, the last stage of a disease which, though not always conspicuous, is always present.

NOTES

1. For an account of the results of this inquiry, see J. B. Tayler, *A Study of Chinese Rural Economy (Chinese Social and Political Science Review*, Vol. VII, Nos. 1 and 2, January and April, 1924). As elsewhere in this study, unless otherwise stated, the dollars are Mexican dollars, equal at par to 1 *s*. 3 *d*. It is possible that the incomes are somewhat understated.

2. F. C. H. Lee and T. Chin, *Village Families in the Vicinity of Peiping*, pp. 23, 53.

3. Buck, *Chinese Farm Economy*, pp. 82–89.

4. Tayler, *op.cit.;* and Mallory, *China, Land of Famine*, pp. 9–11.

5. D. K. Lieu and Chung Min-chen, *Statistics of Farm Land in China (Chinese Economic Journal*, Vol. II, No. 3, March, 1928, pp. 212–13). Their figure of three mow is an average for the whole country, four mow being required in the north and two in the south.

6. For expenditure on food and for diet, see F. C. H. Lee and T. Chin, *op. cit.,* pp. 28–30 (eighty-seven out of one hundred families reported no expenditure on meat); Buck, *op. cit.,* Chapters X and XI, and *An Economic and Social Survey of 150 Farms,* pp. 74–80 (only fifteen out of one hundred and fifty farmers bought any meat during the year). For housing, see Tayler, *op. cit.,* p. 210: "If we take two persons per room as the limit between sufficient accommodation and overcrowding . . . the overcrowding in Chinhsien and Icheng would seem to exceed 90 per cent, to be in the neighbourhood of 50 per cent in Kiangyin and of 20 per cent in Wukiang"; For health and mortality no reliable figures are available, but see C. H. Chao, *A Study on the Rural Population of China,* Department of Agriculture and Forestry, University of Nanking, 1928, summarised in *Nankai Weekly Statistical Service,* March 17, 1930; Paul C. Fugh, *Reconstruction of the Chinese Elementary School Curriculum (Chinese Social and Political Science Review,* Vol. IX, No. 4), where the death-rate of children under five years, in Chinese and missionary families, is compared; the figures of infantile mortality given by Dr. Lenox *(China Journal of Arts and Sciences,* Vol. II, No. 5) on the basis of a study of 4,000 patients in the Peiping Union Medical College; C. M. Chiao and J. Lossing Buck, *The Composition and Growth of Rural Population Groups in China (Chinese Economic Journal,* Vol. II, No. 3, March, 1928), where the average death-rate for the regions studied is given as 27.9 per thousand of population, and the infantile death-rate at 254 per thousand births. For the relation between the size of families and size of holdings, see Tayler, *op. cit.,* pp. 234–5 ("In Chihli the falling off in the size of the family on the small holdings . . . is very marked, a clear indication of economic pressure"); and the following provisional figures collected by the Survey Department, Ting Hsien:

Size of Farm	Number of Families	Number of Persons	Persons per Family
Under 10 mow	174	823	4.7
10–29	167	1,071	6.4
30–49	76	593	7.8
50–69	43	453	10.5
70–99	37	398	10.7
100–149	10	138	13.8
150–299	8	95	11.8
Total	515	3,571	6.9

7. Buck, *An Economic and Social Survey of 150 Farms,* p. 95.

8. The following provisional figures, collected by the Survey Department, Ting Hsien, give some idea, though an imperfect one, of the direct economic losses caused to a group of villages by civil war alone:

Losses of Sixty-two Villages by Civil War in 1928

	Extra Taxation $	Looting $	Total $
Total losses	71,733	39,862	111,595
Loss per village	1,157	643	1,800
Loss per family	6.8	3.8	10.6

Forty out of the sixty-two villages were looted during the war of 1928, involving a total loss of $39,862, or $996.5 per village looted. Four hundred and thirty-five families were affected, and suffered an average loss of $91.6 per family. The number of livestock taken by soldiers was 342, valued at $20,519. In 1927, 7,674 families in the sixty-two villages suffered losses from civil war, estimated to amount to $20,160, or $2.6 per family and $325.2 per village.

9. For Hosie's figures and on the whole subject, see Mallory, *China, Land of Famine*, p. 38.

10. Ta Chen, *Chinese Migrations with Special Reference to Labour Conditions* (Washington, 1928).

11. Co-ching Chu, *Climatic Pulsations in Historic Times in China* (*Geographical Review*, April, 1926).

12. Speech of Mr. Yu Yu-jan, Chairman of the Control Yuan, reported in the *Peking and Tientsin Times*, January 21, 1931; and G. Findlay Andrew, *Manchester Guardian Weekly*, November 21, 1930.

13. See Mallory, *op. cit.*, p. 14.

EDGAR SNOW*

Death and Taxes

A journalistic account is not always a good source for a historian to draw upon, but Edgar Snow's *Red Star over China* has been accepted as one of the most brilliant accounts of China, as he saw it in 1936.

The piece selected gives a vivid though harrowing picture of famine conditions in northwest China.

During the great North-west famine, which lasted roughly for three years, and affected four huge provinces, I visited some of the drought-stricken areas in Suiyuan, on the edge of Mongolia, in June 1929. How many people starved to death in those years I do not accurately know, and probably no one will ever know; it is forgotten now. A conservative semi-official figure of 3,000,000 is often ac-

From Edgar Snow, *Red Star over China,* first revised and enlarged edition (New York: Grove Press, 1968), pp. 225–228. Reprinted by permission of Grove Press, Inc. Copyright © 1938, 1944 by Random House, Inc. Copyright © 1968 by Edgar Snow.

*Edgar Snow is also the author of *Random Notes on Red China* (Cambridge, Mass.: Harvard East Asian Research Center Monograph, 1957) and *The Other Side of the River* (New York: Random House, 1962).

cepted, but I am not inclined to doubt other estimates ranging as high as 6,000,000.

This catastrophe passed hardly noticed in the Western world, or even in the coastal cities of China, but a few courageous men of the China International Famine Relief Commission—many Chinese and some foreigners like Edwards and O. J. Todd and wonderful old Dr. Ingram—risked their skins in those typhus-infested districts to try to salvage a little of the human wreckage. I spent some days with them, passing through cities of death, across a once fertile countryside turned into desert wasteland, through a land of naked horror.

I was twenty-three. I had come to the East looking for the "glamour of the Orient," I suppose. I believe I fancied myself an adventurer, and this excursion to Suiyuan had begun as something like that. But here for the first time in my life I came abruptly upon men who were dying because they had nothing to eat. In those hours of nightmare I spent in Suiyuan I saw thousands of men, women, and children starving to death before my eyes.

Have you ever seen a man—a good honest man who has worked hard, a "law-abiding citizen," doing no serious harm to anyone—when he has had no food for more than a month? It is a most agonizing sight. His dying flesh hangs from him in wrinkled folds; you can clearly see every bone in his body; his eyes stare out unseeing, and even if he is a youth of twenty he moves like an ancient crone, dragging himself from spot to spot. If he has been lucky he has long ago sold his wife and daughters. He has also sold everything he owns—the timber of his house itself, and most of his clothes. Sometimes he has, indeed, even sold the last rag of decency, and he sways there in the scorching sun, his testicles dangling from him like withered olive-seeds—the last grim jest to remind you that this was once a man!

Children are even more pitiable, with their little skeletons bent over and misshapen, their crooked bones, their little arms like twigs, and their purpling bellies, filled with bark and sawdust, protruding like tumours. Women lie slumped in corners, waiting for death, their black blade-like buttocks protruding, their breasts hanging like collapsed sacks. But there are, after all, not many women and girls. Most of them have died or been sold.

I don't mean to dramatize horror. These are things I saw myself and shall never forget. Millions of people died that way in famine, and thousands more still die in China today like that. I saw fresh corpses on the streets of Saratsi, and in the villages I saw shallow graves where victims of famine and disease were laid by the dozens. But these were not the most shocking things after all. The shocking thing was that in many of those towns there were still rich men, rice-hoarders, wheat-hoarders, money-lenders, and landlords, with armed guards to defend them, while they profiteered enormously. The shocking thing was that in the cities—where officials danced or played with sing-song girls—here was grain and food, and had been for months; that in Peking and Tientsin and elsewhere were thousands of tons of wheat and millet, collected (mostly by contributions from abroad) by the Famine Commission, but which could not be shipped to the starving. Why not? Because in the North-west there were some militarists who wanted to hold all of their rolling-stock and would release none of it towards the east, while in the east there were other Kuomintang generals who would send no rolling-stock westward—even to starving people—because they feared it would be seized by their rivals.

While this famine raged the Commission decided to build a big canal (with American funds) to help flood some of the lands baked by drought. The officials gave them every co-operation—and promptly began to buy for a few cents an acre all the lands to be irrigated. A flock of vultures descended upon this benighted country, and purchased from the starving farmers thousands of acres for the taxes in arrears, or for a few coppers, and held it to await tenants and rainy days.

Yet the great majority of those people who died did so without any act of protest!

"Why don't they revolt?" I asked myself. "Why don't they march in a great army and attack the scoundrels who can tax them but cannot feed them, who can seize their lands but cannot repair an irrigation canal? Or why don't they sweep into the great cities, and plunder the wealth of the rascals who buy their daughters and wives, the men who continue to gorge themselves on elaborate thirty-six-course banquets while honest men starve? Why not?"

I was profoundly puzzled by their passivity. For a while I thought nothing would make a Chinese fight.

I was mistaken. The Chinese peasant is not passive; he is not a coward. He will fight when he is given a method, an organization, leadership, a workable programme, hope—*and arms*. The development of "Communism" in China has proved that. Against the above background, therefore, it should not surprise us to see Communists especially popular in the North-west, for conditions there have enjoyed no more fundamental improvement for the mass of the peasantry than elsewhere in China.

V The Rise of the CCP: 1927–1949

(begin reading with Meisner – p. 146 ff.)

From 1923 Borodin and other Communist agents played an exceedingly crucial and decisive role in the development of the KMT and the CCP. The character, composition, and goals of the two parties were, however, very different from each other and led to endless tensions and mutual suspicion. In 1927, just as it began to appear that the Nationalist revolution was succeeding and the revolutionary armies had successfully cleared south and central China of the warlords, the KMT, afraid of a Communist takeover, expelled the CCP and turned against the Russians. The CCP, which had been forced by Moscow to play a subservient role in the revolution, now found itself on the verge of extinction.

By 1928 it appeared that the CCP had been practically crushed and that the KMT had not only emerged victorious but had managed to achieve the first goal of the revolution: the unification of China. Within two decades, however, the KMT was to collapse completely and the CCP was to take over the country and establish the People's Republic.

It is true that during this period China had to fight a war of national survival against Japan and that the KMT, therefore, had little time to carry out its program of reforms. Yet, there is no denying that the KMT, which in fact came to mean Chiang Kai-shek, abandoned revolutionary goals in the interest of preserving power.

The KMT failed to deal with the agrarian question and mobilize the peasantry in the national cause. Chiang Kai-shek's military dictatorship had increasingly to use oppression and naked terror to maintain itself and thereby lost the support of the intelligentsia. Misgovernment, nepotism, corruption, and inflation produced a feeling of demoralization and bitterness which affected not only the common citizen and the peasant masses but also the KMT armies.

The CCP on the other hand, after a decade of failures and setbacks, regrouped itself in Shensi in 1936 and from then on its power and strength grew in a remarkable manner. Since the history of the CCP from 1936 is closely connected with the ascendancy of Mao Tse-tung and his unique interpretations of Marxism-Leninism, this section will try to explain some significant aspects of "Maoism" and to show how Mao used imperialism (Japanese aggression) to heighten a sense of nationalism among the peasant masses and how he created a politically conscious and highly disciplined army and militia, which worked for a social revolution even while fighting the enemy. The high ideals and incorruptibility of the CCP attracted even the nonleftist intellectuals who had been alienated from the KMT.

MAO TSE-TUNG
Poor Peasants: A Revolutionary Force

As early as 1927 Mao Tse-tung (1893–   ), who had then been organizing peasant associations, produced a unique document entitled "Report on an Investigation of the Agrarian Movement in Hunan." (Excerpts from this report are given in the following reading.) The "Report" indicates that Mao had come to the conclusion that the direction of revolutionary movement lay in the country-side and that the peasantry would provide the main force of the revolution. Mao's views were rejected because they deviated so sharply from orthodox Marxism-Leninism. The importance of the "Report" lies in the fact that it reveals many aspects of Mao's "unorthodox" thinking which later came to be enshrined in "ortho-dox" Maoism.

All talk directed against the peasant movement must be speedily set right. All the wrong measures taken by the revolutionary authorities concerning the peasant movement must be speedily changed. Only thus can the future of the revolution be benefited. For the present upsurge of the peasant movement is a colossal event. In a very short time, in

From Mao Tse-tung, "Report on an Investigation of the Peasant Movement in Hunan," in *Selected Works of Mao Tse-tung,* Vol. I (Peking: Foreign Languages Press, 1967), pp. 23–29, 31–34.

China's central, southern and nothern provinces, several hundred million peasants will rise like a mighty storm, like a hurricane, a force so swift and violent that no power, however great, will be able to hold it back. They will smash all the trammels that bind them and rush forward along the road to liberation. They will sweep all the imperialists, warlords, corrupt officials, local tyrants and evil gentry into their graves. Every revolutionary party and every revolutionary comrade will be put to the test, to be accepted or rejected as they decide. There are three alternatives. To march at their head and lead them? To trail behind them, gesticulating and criticizing? Or to stand in their way and oppose them? Every Chinese is free to choose, but events will force you to make the choice quickly.

The main targets of attack by the peasants are the local tyrants, the evil gentry and the lawless landlords, but in passing they also hit out against patriarchal ideas and institutions, against the corrupt officials in the cities and against bad practices and customs in the rural areas. In force and momentum the attack is tempestuous; those who bow before it survive and those who resist perish. As a result, the privileges which the feudal landlords enjoyed for thousands of years are being shattered to pieces. Every bit of the dignity and prestige built up by the landlords is being swept into the dust. With the collapse of the power of the landlords, the peasant associations have now become the sole organs of authority and the popular slogan "All power to the peasant associations" has become a reality. . . . The local tyrants, evil gentry and lawless landlords have been deprived of all right to speak, and none of them dares even mutter dissent. . . .

The peasants' revolt disturbed the gentry's sweet dreams. When the news from the countryside reached the cities, it caused immediate uproar among the gentry. Soon after my arrival in Changsha, I met all sorts of people and picked up a good deal of gossip. From the middle social strata upwards to the Kuomintang right-wingers, there was not a single person who did not sum up the whole business in the phrase, "It's terrible!" Under the impact of the views of the "It's terrible!" school then flooding the city, even quite revolutionary-minded people became down-hearted as they pictured the events in the countryside in their mind's eye; and they were unable to deny the word "terrible." Even quite progressive people said, "Though terrible, it is inevitable in a revolution." In short, nobody could altogether deny the word "terrible." But, as already mentioned, the fact is that the great peasant masses have risen to fulfill their historic mission and that the forces of rural democracy have risen to overthrow the forces of rural feudalism. The patriarchal-feudal class of local tyrants, evil gentry and lawless landlords has formed the basis of autocratic government for thousands of years and is the cornerstone of imperialism, warlordism and corrupt officialdom. To overthrow these feudal forces is the real objective of the national revolution. In a few months the peasants have accomplished what Dr. Sun Yat-sen wanted, but failed, to accomplish in the forty years he devoted to the national revolution. This is a marvellous feat never before achieved, not just in forty, but in thousands of years. It's fine. It is not "terrible" at all. It is anything but "terrible." "It's terrible!" is obviously a theory for combating the rise of the peasants in the interests of the landlords; it is obviously a theory of the landlord class for preserving the old order of feudalism and obstructing the establishment of the new order of democracy; it is obviously a counter-revolutionary theory. No revolutionary comrade should echo this nonsense. If your revolutionary viewpoint is firmly established and if you have been to the villages and looked around, you will undoubtedly feel thrilled as never before. Countless thousands of the enslaved—the peasants—are striking down the enemies who battened on their flesh. What the peasants are doing is absolutely right; what they are doing is fine! "It's fine!" is the theory of the peasants and of all other revolutionaries. Every revolutionary comrade should know that the national revolution requires a great change in the countryside. The Revolution of 1911 did not bring about this change, hence its failure. This change is now taking place, and it is an important factor for the completion of the revolution. Every revolutionary comrade must support it, or he will be taking the stand of counter-revolution.

. . . Doing whatever they like and turning everything upside down, they have created a kind of terror in the countryside. This is what some people call "going too far," or "exceeding the proper limits in righting a wrong," or "really too much." Such talk may seem plausible, but in fact it is wrong. First, the local tyrants, evil gentry and lawless landlords have themselves driven the peasants to this. For ages they have used their power to tyrannize over the peasants and trample them underfoot; that is why the peasants have reacted so strongly. The most violent revolts and the most serious disorders have invariably occurred in places where the local tyrants, evil gentry and lawless landlords perpetrated the worst outrages. The peasants are clear-sighted. Who is bad and who is not, who is the worst and who is not quite so vicious, who deserves severe punishment and who deserves to be let off lightly—the peasants keep clear accounts, and very seldom has the punishment exceeded the crime. Secondly, a revolution is not a dinner party, or writing an essay, or painting a picture, or doing embroidery; it cannot be so refined, so leisurely and gentle, so temperate, kind, courteous, restrained and magnanimous. A revolution is an insurrection, an act of violence by which one class overthrows another. A rural revolution is a revolution by which the peasantry overthrows the power of the feudal landlord class. Without using the greatest force, the peasants cannot possibly overthrow the deep-rooted authority of the landlords which has lasted for thousands of years. The rural areas need a mighty revolutionary upsurge, for it alone can rouse the people in their millions to become a powerful force. . . . To put it bluntly, it is necessary to create terror for a while in every rural area, or otherwise it would be impossible to suppress the activities of the counter-revolutionaries in the countryside or overthrow the authority of the gentry. Proper limits have to be exceeded in order to right a wrong, or else the wrong cannot be righted.

After joining, the rich peasants are not keen on doing any work for the associations. They remain inactive throughout.

How about the middle peasants? Theirs is a vacillating attitude. They think that the revolution will not bring them much good. They have rice cooking in their pots and no creditors knocking on their doors at midnight. They, too, judging a thing by whether it ever existed before, knit their brows and think to themselves, "Can the peasant association really last?" . . . They show up better in the associations than the rich peasants but are not as yet very enthusiastic; they still want to wait and see. It is essential for the peasant associations to get the middle peasants to join and to do a good deal more explanatory work among them.

The poor peasants have always been the main force in the bitter fight in the countryside. They have fought militantly through the two periods of underground work and of open activity. They are the most responsive to Communist Party leadership. They are deadly enemies of the camp of the local tyrants and evil gentry and attack it without the slightest hesitation. . . . This great mass of poor peasants, or altogether 70 per cent of the rural population, are the backbone of the peasant associations, the vanguard in the overthrow of the feudal forces and the heroes who have performed the great revolutionary task which for long years was left undone. . . . Leadership by the poor peasants is absolutely necessary. Without the poor peasants there would be no revolution. To deny their role is to deny the revolution. To attack them is to attack the revolution. They have never been wrong on the general direction of the revolution. They have discredited the local tyrants and evil gentry. They have beaten down the local tyrants and evil gentry, big and small, and kept them underfoot. Many of their deeds in the period of revolutionary action, which were labelled as "going too far," were in fact the very things the revolution required. . . . They themselves are energetically prohibiting gambling and suppressing banditry. Where the peasant association is powerful, gambling has stopped altogether and banditry has vanished. In some places it is literally true that people do not take any articles left by the wayside and that doors are not bolted at night.

MAO TSE-TUNG, *ET AL.*
Imperialism and China

It is interesting to compare this piece written in 1939 with K'ang Yu-wei's speech, "The Nation Is in Danger" (see Section I), delivered in 1898. Where K'ang concluded that the defect lay mainly in the inertia of China's own intellectuals, who had not taken the trouble to save their country, Mao puts the blame almost entirely on others, the "imperialist powers."

(1) The imperialist powers have waged many wars of aggression against China, for instance, the Opium War launched by Britain in 1840, the war launched by the Anglo-French allied forces in 1857,[1] the Sino-French War of 1884,[2] the Sino-Japanese War of 1894, and the war launched by the allied forces of the eight powers in 1900.[3] After defeating China in war, they not only occupied many neighbouring countries formerly under her protection, but seized or "leased" parts of her territory. For instance, Japan occupied Taiwan and the Penghu Islands and "leased" the port of Lushun, Britain seized Hongkong and France "leased" Kwangchowwan. In addition to annexing territory,

---

From Mao Tse-tung, "The Chinese Revolution and the Chinese Communist Party," in *Selected Works of Mao Tse-tung,* Vol. II (Peking: Foreign Languages Press, 1967), pp. 311–312. This long article was originally written by Mao Tse-tung and other members of the CCP as a textbook in 1939.

they exacted huge indemnities. Thus heavy blows were struck at China's huge feudal empire.

(2) The imperialist powers have forced China to sign numerous unequal treaties by which they have acquired the right to station land and sea forces and exercise consular jurisdiction in China,[4] and they have carved up the whole country into imperialist spheres of influence.[5]

(3) The imperialist powers have gained control of all the important trading ports in China by these unequal treaties and have marked off areas in many of these ports as concessions under their direct administration.[6] They have also gained control of China's customs, foreign trade and communications (sea, land, inland water and air). Thus they have been able to dump their goods in China, turn her into a market for their industrial products, and at the same time subordinate her agriculture to their imperialist needs.

(4) The imperialist powers operate many enterprises in both light and heavy industry in China in order to utilize her raw materials and cheap labour on the spot, and they thereby directly exert economic pressure on China's national industry and obstruct the development of her productive forces.

(5) The imperialist powers monopolize China's banking and finance by extending loans to the Chinese government and establishing banks in China. Thus they have not only overwhelmed China's national capitalism in commodity competition, they have also secured a stranglehold on her banking and finance.

(6) The imperialist powers have established a network of comprador and merchant-usurer exploitation right across China, from the trading ports to the remote hinterland, and have created a comprador and merchant-usurer class in their service, so as to facilitate their exploitation of the masses of the Chinese peasantry and other sections of the people.

(7) The imperialist powers have made the feudal landlord class as well as the comprador class the main props of their rule in China. Imperialism "first allies itself with the ruling strata of the previous social structure, with the feudal lords and the trading and moneylending bourgeoisie, against the majority of the people. Everywhere imperialism attempts to preserve and to perpetuate all those precapitalist forms of exploitation (especially in the villages) which serve as the basis for the existence of its reactionary allies."[7] "Imperialism, with all its financial and military might, is the force in China that supports,

inspires, fosters and preserves the feudal survivals, together with their entire bureaucratic-militarist superstructure.''[8]

(8) The imperialist powers supply the reactionary government with large quantities of munitions and a host of military advisers, in order to keep the warlords fighting among themselves and to suppress the Chinese people.

(9) Furthermore, the imperialist powers have never slackened their efforts to poison the minds of the Chinese people. This is their policy of cultural aggression. And it is carried out through missionary work, through establishing hospitals and schools, publishing newspapers and including Chinese students to study abroad. Their aim is to train intellectuals who will serve their interests and to dupe the people.

(10) Since September 18, 1931, the large-scale invasion of Japanese imperialism has turned a big chunk of semi-colonial China into a Japanese colony.

These facts represent the other aspect of the change that has taken place since the imperialist penetration of China—the blood-stained picture of feudal China being reduced to semi-feudal, semi-colonial and colonial China.

NOTES

1. From 1856 to 1860 Britain and France jointly waged a war of aggression against China, with the United States and tsarist Russia supporting them from the side-lines. The government of the Ching Dynasty was then devoting all its energies to suppressing the peasant revolution of the Taiping Heavenly Kingdom and adopted a policy of passive resistance towards the foreign aggressors. The Anglo-French forces occupied such major cities as Canton, Tientsin and Peking, plundered and burned down the Yuan Ming Yuan Palace in Peking and forced the Ching government to conclude the Treaties of Tientsin and Peking. Their main provisions included the opening of Tientsin, Newchwang, Tengchow, Taiwan, Tamsui, Chaochow, Chiungchow, Nanking, Chinkiang, Kiukiang and Hankow as treaty ports, and the granting to foreigners of special privileges for travel, missionary activities and inland navigation in China's interior. From then on, the foreign forces of aggression spread through all China's coastal provinces and penetrated deep into the hinterland.

2. In 1882–83, the French aggressors invaded the northern part of Indo-China. In 1884–85 they extended their war of aggression to the Chinese provinces of Kwangsi, Taiwan, Fukien and Chekiang. Despite the victories gained in this war, the corrupt Ching government signed the humiliating Treaty of Tientsin.

3. In 1900 eight imperialist powers, Britain, the United States, Germany, France, tsarist Russia, Japan, Italy and Austria, sent a joint force to attack China in their attempt to suppress the Yi Ho Tuan Movement of the Chinese people against aggression. The Chinese people resisted heroically. The allied forces of the eight powers captured Taku and occupied Tientsin and Peking. In 1901 the Ching government concluded a treaty with the eight imperialist countries; its main provisions were that China had to pay those countries the huge sum of 450 million taels of silver as war reparations and grant them the

special privilege of stationing troops in Peking and in the area from Peking to Tientsin and Shanhaikuan.

4. Consular jurisdiction was one of the special privileges provided in the unequal treaties which the imperialist powers forced on the governments of old China—beginning with the supplementary treaty to the Sino-British Treaty of Nanking, signed at Humen (the Bogue) in 1843, and with the Sino-American Treaty of Wanghia in 1844. It meant that, if a national of any country enjoying the privilege of consular jurisdiction in China became a defendant in a lawsuit, civil or criminal, he was not to be tried by a Chinese court but by the consul of his own country.

5. Spheres of influence were different parts of China marked off at the end of the 19th century by the imperialist powers that committed aggression against China. Each of these powers marked off those areas which fell within its economic and military influence. Thus, the provinces in the lower and middle Yangtse valley were specified as the British sphere of influence; Yunnan, Kwangtung and Kwangsi as the French; Shantung as the German sphere; Fukien as the Japanese; and the three northeastern provinces (the present provinces of Liaoning, Kirin and Heilungkiang) as the tsarist Russian sphere. After the Russo-Japanese War of 1905 the southern part of the three northeastern provinces came under Japanese influence.

6. The foreign concessions were areas which the imperialist powers seized in the treaty ports after compelling the Ching government to open these ports. In these so-called concessions they enforced an imperialist system of colonial rule entirely independent of Chinese law and administration. Through those concessions, the imperialists exercised direct or indirect political and economic control over the Chinese feudal land comprador regime. During the revolution of 1924–27 the revolutionary people led by the Chinese Communist Party started a movement to abolish the concessions, and in January 1927 they took over the British concessions in Hankow and Kiukiang. However, the imperialists retained various concessions after Chiang Kai-shek betrayed the revolution.

7. "The Theses on the Revolutionary Movement in Colonial and Semi-Colonial Countries" adopted by the Sixth Comintern Congress, stenographic record of the Sixth Comintern Congress, issue No. 6, Russ. ed., Moscow, 1929, p. 128.

8. J. V. Stalin, "The Revolution in China and the Tasks of the Comintern," *Works*, Eng. ed., FLPH, Moscow, 1954, Vol. IX, p. 292.

MAO TSE-TUNG
Rectify the Party's Style of Work

In a speech delivered in February 1942, at the opening of the Party School of the Central Committee of the CCP, Mao Tse-tung discussed the evils of "sectarianism." Excerpts from this speech quoted below reveal Mao's attitude toward intellectuals, his con-

---

From Mao Tse-tung, "Rectify the Party's Style of Work," in *Selected Works of Mao Tse-tung*, Vol. III (Peking: Foreign Languages Press, 1967), pp. 35–51.

cept of theory and practice, and his emphasis on unity of the army, the Party, and the masses.

The Party School opens today and I wish it every success.

I would like to say something about the problem of our Party's style of work. . . .

What is the problem now facing our Party? . . . It is the fact that there is something in the minds of a number of our comrades which strikes one as not quite right, not quite proper.

In other words, there is still something wrong with our style of study, with our style in the Party's internal and external relations. . . . By something wrong with the style of study we mean the malady of subjectivism. By something wrong with our style of Party relations we mean the malady of sectarianism. . . .

Subjectivism is an improper style of study; it is opposed to Marxism-Leninism and is incompatible with the Communist Party. What we want is the Marxist-Leninist style of study. What we call style of study means not just style of study in the schools but in the whole Party. It is a question of the method of thinking of comrades in our leading bodies, of all cadres and Party members, a question of our attitude towards Marxism-Leninism, of the attitude of all Party comrades in their work. As such, it is a question of extraordinary, indeed of primary, importance.

Certain muddled ideas find currency among many people. There are, for instance, muddled ideas about what is a theorist, what is an intellectual and what is meant by linking theory and practice.

Let us first ask, is the theoretical level of our Party high or low? Recently more Marxist-Leninist works have been translated and more people have been reading them. That is a very good thing. But can we therefore say that the theoretical level of our Party has been greatly raised? True, the level is now somewhat higher than before. But our theoretical front is very much out of harmony with the rich content of the Chinese revolutionary movement, and a comparison of the two shows that the theoretical side is lagging far behind. . . . We have read a great many Marxist-Leninist books, but can we claim, then, that we have theorists? We cannot. For Marxism-Leninism is the theory created by Marx, Engels, Lenin and Stalin on the basis of practice, their general conclusion drawn from historical and revolutionary reality. If we merely read their works but do not proceed to study the realities of

China's history and revolution in the light of their theory or do not make any effort to think through China's revolutionary practice carefully in terms of theory, we should not be so presumptuous as to call ourselves Marxist theorists. Our achievements on the theoretical front will be very poor indeed if, as members of the Communist Party of China, we close our eyes to China's problems and can only memorize isolated conclusions or principles from Marxist writings. . . .

Our comrades in the Party School should not regard Marxist theory as lifeless dogma. It is necessary to master Marxist theory and apply it, master it for the sole purpose of applying it. . . . Our Party School should also lay down the rule to grade students good or poor according to how they look at China's problems after they have studied Marxism-Leninism, according to whether or not they see the problems clearly and whether or not they see them at all.

Next let us talk about the question of the "intellectuals." Since China is a semi-colonial, semi-feudal country and her culture is not well developed, intellectuals are particularly treasured. On this question of the intellectuals, the Central Committee of the Party made the decision[1] over two years ago that we should win over the great numbers of intellectuals and, insofar as they are revolutionary and willing to take part in the resistance to Japan, welcome them one and all. It is entirely right for us to esteem intellectuals, for without revolutionary intellectuals the revolution cannot triumph. But we all know there are many intellectuals who fancy themselves very learned and assume airs of erudition without realizing that such airs are bad and harmful and hinder their own progress. They ought to be aware of the truth that actually many so-called intellectuals are, relatively speaking, most ignorant and the workers and peasants sometimes know more than they do. Here some will say, "Ha! You are turning things upside down and talking nonsense." *(Laughter.)* But, comrades, don't get excited; there is some sense in what I am saying.

What is knowledge? Ever since class society came into being the world has had only two kinds of knowledge, knowledge of the struggle for production and knowledge of the class struggle. Natural science and social science are the crystallizations of these two kinds of knowledge, and philosophy is the generalization and summation of the knowledge of nature and the knowledge of society. Is there any other kind of knowledge? No. . . . What sort of knowledge is the students' book-learning? Even supposing all their knowledge is truth, it is still not knowledge acquired through their own personal experience, but consists of theories set down by their predecessors in summarizing experience of the struggle for production and of the class struggle. . . . Therefore, I advise those who have only book-learning but as yet no contact with reality, and also those with little practical experience, to realize their own shortcomings and become a little more modest.

How can those who have only book-learning be turned into intellectuals in the true sense? The only way is to get them to take part in practical work and become practical workers, to get those engaged in theoretical work to study important practical problems. In this way our aim can be attained.

What I have said will probably make some people angry. They will say, "According to your explanation, even Marx would not be regarded as an intellectual." I say they are wrong. Marx took part in the practice of the revolutionary movement and also created revolutionary theory. . . . He studied nature, history and proletarian revolution and created dialectical materialism, historical materialism and the theory of proletarian revolution. Thus Marx became a most completely developed intellectual, representing the acme of human wisdom; he was fundamentally different from those who have only book-learning. . . . In our Party there are many comrades who can learn to do this kind of theoretical research; most of them are intelligent and promising and we should value them. But they must follow correct principles and not repeat the mistake of the past. They must discard dogmatism and not confine themselves to ready-made phrases in books. . . .

On the other hand, our comrades who are engaged in practical work will also come to grief if they misuse their experience. True, these people are often rich in experience, which is very valuable, but it is very dangerous if they rest content with their own experience. They must realize that their knowledge is mostly perceptual and partial and that they lack rational and comprehensive knowledge; in other words, they lack theory and their knowledge, too, is relatively incomplete. Without comparatively complete knowledge it is impossible to do revolutionary work well.

Thus, there are two kinds of incomplete knowledge, one is ready-made knowledge found in books and the other is knowledge that is mostly perceptual and partial; both are one-sided. Only an integration of the two can yield knowledge that is sound and relatively complete.

In order to study theory, however, our cadres of working-class and peasant origin must first acquire an elementary education. Without it they cannot learn Marxist-Leninist theory. Having acquired it, they can study Marxism-Leninism at any time. In my childhood I never attended a Marxist-Leninist school and was taught only such things as, "The Master said: 'How pleasant it is to learn and constantly review what one has learned.' "[2] Though this teaching material was antiquated, it did me some good because from it I learned to read. Nowadays we no longer study the Confucian classics but such new subjects as modern Chinese, history, geography and elementary natural science, which, once learned, are useful everywhere. The Central Committee of our Party now emphatically requires that our cadres of working-class and peasant origin should obtain an elementary education because they can then take up any branch of study—politics, military science or economics. Otherwise, for all their rich experience they will never be able to study theory.

It follows that to combat subjectivism . . . those with book-learning must develop in the direction of practice. . . . Those experienced in work must take up the study of theory and must read seriously. . . . There are two kinds of subjectivism in our Party, dogmatism and empiricism. Each sees only a part and not the whole. . . .

However, of the two kinds of subjectivism, dogmatism is still the greater danger in our Party. For dogmatists can easily assume a Marxist guise to bluff, capture and make servitors of cadres of working-class and peasant origin who cannot easily see through them; they can also bluff and ensnare the naive youth. . . .

Besides muddled ideas about the "theorist" and the "intellectual," there is a muddled idea among many comrades about "linking theory and practice," a phrase they have on their lips every day. They talk constantly about "linking," but actually they mean "separating," because they make no effort at linking. How is Marxist-Leninist theory to be linked with the practice of the Chinese revolution? To use a common expression, it is by "shooting the arrow at the target." As the arrow is to the target, so is Marxism-Leninism to the Chinese revolution. Some comrades, however, are "shooting without a target," shooting at random, and such people are liable to harm the revolution. Others merely stroke the arrow fondly, exclaiming, "What a fine arrow! What a fine arrow!," but never want to shoot it. These people are only connoisseurs of curios and have virtually nothing to do with the revolution. The arrow of Marxism-Leninism must be used to shoot at the target of the Chinese revolution. . . .

Let me now speak about the question of sectarianism.

Having been steeled for twenty years, our Party is no longer dominated by sectarianism. Remnants of sectarianism, however, are still found both in the Party's internal relations and in its external relations. Sectarian tendencies in internal relations lead to exclusiveness towards comrades inside the Party and hinder inner-Party unity and solidarity, while sectarian tendencies in external relations lead to exclusiveness towards people outside the Party and hinder the Party in its task of uniting the whole people. . . .

What are the remnants of inner-Party sectarianism? They are mainly as follows:

First, the assertion of "independence." Some comrades see only the interests of the part and not the whole; they always put undue stress on that part of the work for which they themselves are responsible and always wish to subordinate the interests of the whole to the interests of their own part. They do not understand the Party's system of democratic centralism; they do not realize that the Communist Party not only needs democracy but needs centralization even more. They forget the system of democratic centralism in which the minority is subordinate to the majority, the lower level to the higher level, the part to the whole and the entire membership to the Central Committee. . . .

Those who assert this kind of "independence" are usually wedded to the doctrine of "me first" and are generally wrong on the question of the relationship between the individual and the Party. Although in words they profess respect for the Party, in practice they put themselves first and the Party second. . . . We must build a centralized, unified Party and make a clean sweep of all unprincipled factional struggles. We must combat individualism and sectarianism so as to enable our whole Party to march in step and fight for one common goal.

Cadres from the outside and those from the locality must unite and combat sectarian tendencies. Very careful attention must be given to the relations between outside and local cadres because many anti-Japanese base areas were established only after the arrival of the Eighth Route Army or the New Fourth Army and much of the local work developed only after the arrival of outside cadres. . . . Generally speaking, in places where outside cadres are in charge, it is they who should bear the main responsibility if their relations with the local cadres are not good. And the chief comrades in charge should bear greater responsibility. . . . Some people look down on the local cadres and ridicule them, saying, "What do these locals know? Clodhoppers!" Such people utterly fail to understand the importance of local cadres; they know neither the latter's strong points nor their own weaknesses and adopt an incorrect, sectarian attitude. . . .

The same applies to the relationship between cadres in army service and other cadres working in the locality. They must be completely united and must oppose sectarian tendencies. . . .

The same applies to the relationship among different army units, different localities and different departments. We must oppose the tendency towards selfish departmentalism by which the interests of one's own unit are looked after to the exclusion of those of others.

Another problem is the relationship between old and new cadres. Since the beginning of the War of Resistance, our Party has grown enormously, and large numbers of new cadres have emerged; that is a very good thing. In his report to the Eighteenth Congress of the Communist Party of the Soviet Union (B.), Comrade Stalin said, " . . . there are never enough old cadres, there are far less than required, and they are already partly going out of commission owing to the operation of the laws of nature." . . . If our Party does not have a great many new cadres working in unity and co-operation with the old cadres, our cause will come to a stop. All old cadres, therefore, should welcome the new ones with the utmost enthusiasm and show them the warmest solicitude.

The remnants of sectarianism must be eliminated from the Party's external as well as its internal relations. The reason is this: we cannot defeat the enemy by merely uniting the comrades throughout the Party, we can defeat the enemy only by uniting the people throughout the country. For twenty years the Communist Party of China has done great and arduous work in the cause of uniting the people of the whole country, and the achievements in this work since the outbreak of the War of Resistance are even greater than in the past. This does not mean, however, that all our comrades already have a correct style in dealing with the masses and are free from sectarian tendencies. No. In fact, sectarian tendencies still exist among a number of comrades, and in some cases to a very serious degree. After reading a few Marxist books, such comrades become more arrogant instead of more modest, and invariably dismiss others as no good without realizing that in fact their own knowledge is only half-baked. Our comrades must realize the truth that Communist Party members are at all times a minority as compared with non-Party people. . . . What reason can we then have for not co-operating with non-Party people? As regards all those who wish to co-operate with us or might co-operate with us, we have only the duty of co-operating and absolutely no right to shut them out. . . . Thus any action divorcing us from the masses has no justification at all and is simply the mischievous result of the sectarian ideas some of our comrades have themselves concocted. As such sectarianism remains very serious among some of our comrades and still obstructs the application of the Party line, we should carry out extensive education within the Party to meet this problem. Above all, we should make our cadres really understand how serious the problem is and how utterly impossible it is to overthrow the enemy and attain the goal of the revolution unless Party members unite with the non-Party cadres and with non-Party people.

All sectarian ideas are subjectivist and are incomparable with the real needs of the revolution; hence the struggle against sectarianism and the struggle against subjectivism should go on simultaneously.

NOTES

1. This was the decision on recruiting intellectuals adopted by the Central Committee of the Communist Party of China in December 1939, which is printed under the title "Recruit Large Numbers of Intellectuals" in the *Selected Works of Mao Tse-tung*, Vol. II.

2. This is the opening sentence of the *Confucian Analects*, a record of the dialogues of Confucius and his disciples.

MAO TSE-TUNG
The Japanese War and Peasant Nationalism

The Japanese War which exposed the weaknesses in the KMT government and undermined the Chungking regime provided an excellent opportunity for the CCP to awaken a sense of nationalism among the peasant masses and win their support. It is this political mobilization of the masses which helped the CCP not only to gain ultimate political victory but also to successfully introduce social and economic changes in the countryside.

From Mao Tse-tung, "On Protracted War," in *Selected Works of Mao Tse-tung*, Vol. II (Peking: Foreign Languages Press, 1967), pp. 154–155, 186–187. "On Protracted War" is a collection of a series of lectures delivered by Mao Tse-tung from May 26 to June 3, 1938, at the Yenan Association for the Study of War of Resistance Against Japan.

A national revolutionary war as great as ours cannot be won without extensive and thoroughgoing political mobilization. Before the anti-Japanese war there was no political mobilization for resistance to Japan, and this was a great drawback, as a result of which China has already lost a move to the enemy. After the war began, political mobilization was very far from extensive, let alone thoroughgoing. It was the enemy's gunfire and the bombs dropped by enemy aeroplanes that brought news of the war to the great majority of the people. That was also a kind of mobilization, but it was done for us by the enemy, we did not do it ourselves. Even now the people in the remoter regions beyond the noise of the guns are carrying on quietly as usual. This situation must change, or otherwise we cannot win in our life-and-death struggle. We must never lose another move to the enemy; on the contrary, we must make full use of this move, political mobilization, to get the better of him. This move is crucial; it is indeed of primary importance, while our inferiority in weapons and other things is only secondary. The mobilization of the common people throughout the country will create a vast sea in which to drown the enemy, create the conditions that will make up for our inferiority in arms and other things, and create the prerequisites for overcoming every difficulty in the war. To win victory, we must persevere in the War of Resistance, in the united front and in the protracted war. But all these are inseparable from the mobilization of the common people. To wish for victory and yet neglect political mobilization is like wishing to "go south by driving the chariot north," and the result would inevitably be to forfeit victory.

What does political mobilization mean? First, it means telling the army and the people about the political aim of the war. It is necessary for every soldier and civilian to see why the war must be fought and how it concerns him. The political aim of the war is "to drive out Japanese imperialism and build a new China of freedom and equality"; we must proclaim this aim to everybody, to all soldiers and civilians, before we can create an anti-Japanese upsurge and unite hundreds of millions as one man to contribute their all to the war. Secondly, it is not enough merely to explain the aim to them; the steps and policies for its attainment must also be given, that is, there must be a political programme. We already have the Ten-Point Programme for Resisting Japan and Saving the Nation and also the Programme of Armed Resistance and National Reconstruction; we should popularize both of them in the army and among the people and mobilize everyone to carry them out. Without a clear-cut, concrete political programme it is impossible to mobilize all the armed forces and the whole people to carry the war against Japan through to the end. Thirdly, how should we mobilize them? By word of mouth, by leaflets and bulletins, by newspapers, books and pamphlets, through plays and films, through schools, through the mass organizations and through our cadres. What has been done so far in the Kuomintang areas is only a drop in the ocean, and moreover it has been done in a manner ill-suited to the people's tastes and in a spirit uncongenial to them; this must be drastically changed. Fourthly, to mobilize once is not enough; political mobilization for the War of Resistance must be continuous. Our job is not to recite our political programme to the people, for nobody will listen to such recitations; we must link the political mobilization for the war with developments in the war and with the life of the soldiers and the people, and make it a continuous movement. This is a matter of immense importance on which our victory in the war primarily depends. . . .

The richest source of power to wage war lies in the masses of the people. It is mainly because of the unorganized state of the Chinese masses that Japan dares to bully us. When this defect is remedied, then the Japanese aggressor, like a mad bull crashing into a ring of flames, will be surrounded by hundreds of millions of our people standing upright, the mere sound of their voices will strike terror into him, and he will be burned to death. China's armies must have an uninterrupted flow of reinforcements, and the abuses of press-ganging and of buying substitutes,[1] which now exist at the lower levels, must immediately be banned and replaced by widespread and enthusiastic political mobilization, which will make it easy to enlist millions of men. We now have great difficulties in raising money for the war, but once the people are mobilized, finances too will cease to be a problem. Why should a country as large and populous as China suffer from lack of funds? The army must become one with the people so that they see it as their own army. Such an army will be invincible, and an imperialist power like Japan will be no match for it.

Many people think that it is wrong methods that make for strained relations between officers and men and between the army and the people, but I always tell them that it is a question of basic attitude (or basic principle), of having respect for the soldiers and the people. It is from this attitude that the various policies, methods and forms ensue. If we depart from this attitude, then the policies, methods and forms will certainly be wrong, and the relations between officers and men and between the army and the people are bound to be unsatisfactory. Our three major principles for the army's political work are, first, unity between officers and men; second, unity between the army and the people; and third, the disintegration of the enemy forces. To apply these principles effectively, we must start with this basic attitude of respect for the soldiers and the people, and of respect for human dignity of prisoners of war once they have laid down their arms. Those who take all this as a technical matter and not one of basic attitude are indeed wrong, and they should correct their view. . . .

In all our work we must persevere in the Anti-Japanese National United Front as the general policy. For only with this policy can we persevere in the War of Resistance and in protracted warfare, bring about a widespread and profound improvement in the relations between officers and men and between the army and the people, arouse to the full the initiative and enthusiasm of the entire army and the entire people in the fight for the defence of all the territory still in our hands and for the recovery of what we have lost, and so win final victory.

This question of the political mobilization of the army and the people is indeed of the greatest importance. We have dwelt on it at the risk of repetition precisely because victory is impossible without it. *There are, of course, many other conditions indispensable to victory, but political mobilization is the most fundamental.** The Anti-Japanese National United Front is a united front of the whole army and the whole people, it is certainly not a united front merely of the headquarters and members of a few political parties; our basic objective in initiating the Anti-Japanese National United Front is to mobilize the whole army and the whole people to participate in it.

*Italics added.

NOTE

1. The Kuomintang expanded its army by press-ganging. Its military and police seized people everywhere, roping them up and treating them like convicts. Those who had money would bribe the Kuomintang officials or pay for substitutes.

MAO TSE-TUNG
A Rural Base for the Revolution

Here is another aspect of Maoism—Mao's revolutionary strategy which accepts that the revolutionary force resides in the countryside and that revolutionary rural areas encircle the cities which, though targets for the revolution, are nonrevolutionary. — *indeed, centers of reaction or their superstructure*

In the War of Resistance a section of the big landlord class and big bourgeoisie, represented by Wang Ching-wei, has turned traitor and deserted to the enemy. Consequently, the anti-Japanese people cannot but regard these big bourgeois elements who have betrayed our national interests as one of the targets of the revolution.

It is evident, then, that the enemies of the Chinese revolution are very powerful. They include not only powerful imperialists and powerful feudal forces, but also, at times, the bourgeois reactionaries who collaborate with the imperialist and feudal forces to oppose the people. Therefore, it is wrong to underestimate the strength of the enemies of the revolutionary Chinese people.

In the face of such enemies, the Chinese revolution cannot be other than protracted and ruthless. With such powerful enemies, the revolutionary forces cannot be built up and tempered into a power capable of crushing them except over a long period of time. With enemies who so ruthlessly suppress the Chinese revolution, the revolutionary forces cannot hold their own positions, let alone capture those of the enemy, unless they steel themselves and display their tenacity to the full. It is therefore wrong to think that the forces of the Chinese revolution can be built up in the twinkling of an eye, or that China's revolutionary struggle can triumph overnight.

In the face of such enemies, the principal means or form of the Chinese revolution must be armed struggle, not peaceful struggle. For our enemies have made peaceful activity impossible for the Chinese people and have deprived them of all political freedom and democratic

---

From Mao Tse-tung, "The Chinese Revolution and the Chinese Communist Party," in *Selected Works of Mao Tse-tung*, Vol. II (Peking: Foreign Languages Press, 1967), pp. 316–317. *The Chinese Revolution and the Chinese Communist Party* was a textbook written by Mao Tse-tung with the help of other CCP members in 1939.

rights. Stalin says, "In China the armed revolution is fighting the armed counter-revolution. That is one of the specific features and one of the advantages of the Chinese revolution."[1] This formulation is perfectly correct. Therefore, it is wrong to belittle armed struggle, revolutionary war, guerrilla war and army work.

In the face of such enemies, there arises the question of revolutionary base areas. *Since China's key cities have long been occupied by the powerful imperialists and their reactionary Chinese allies, it is imperative for the revolutionary ranks to turn the backward villages into advanced, consolidated base areas, into great military, political, economic and cultural bastions of the revolution from which to fight their vicious enemies who are using the cities for attacks on the rural districts,* and in this way gradually to achieve the complete victory of the revolution through protracted fighting; it is imperative for them to do so if they do not wish to compromise with imperialism and its lackeys but are determined to fight on, and if they intend to build up and temper their forces, and avoid decisive battles with a powerful enemy while their own strength is inadequate. Such being the case, *victory in the Chinese revolution can be won first in the rural areas, and this is possible because China's economic development is uneven* (her economy not being a unified capitalist economy), *because her territory is extensive* (which gives the revolutionary forces room to manoeuvre), *because the counter-revolutionary camp is disunited and full of contradictions, and because the struggle of the peasants who are the main force in the revolution is led by the Communist Party,* the party of the proletariat; but on the other hand, these very circumstances make the revolution uneven and render the task of winning complete victory protracted and arduous. Clearly then the protracted revolutionary struggle in the revolutionary base areas consists mainly in peasant guerrilla warfare led by the Chinese Communist Party. Therefore, it is wrong to ignore the necessity of using rural districts as revolutionary base areas, to neglect painstaking work among the peasants, and to neglect guerrilla warfare.

However, stressing armed struggle does not mean abandoning other forms of struggle; on the contrary, armed struggle cannot succeed unless co-ordinated with other forms of struggle. And stressing the work in the rural base areas does not mean abandoning our work in the cities and in the other vast rural areas which are still under the enemy's rule;

*All italics added.

on the contrary, without the work in the cities and in these other rural areas, our own rural base areas would be isolated and the revolution would suffer defeat. Moreover, the final objective of the revolution is the capture of the cities, the enemy's main bases, and this objective cannot be achieved without adequate work in the cities.

NOTE

1. J. V. Stalin, "The Prospects of the Revolution in China," *Works*, English ed., FLPH, Moscow, 1954, Vol. VIII, p. 379.

LIU SHAO-CH'I
How to Be a Good Communist

Liu Shao-ch'i, Chairman of the People's Republic of China since 1959 and for a long time considered the successor to Mao Tse-tung, was purged from authority in 1967 during the "cultural revolution." A leading expert on the theory and practice of party organization, Liu Shao-ch'i had, however, played an important role in the development of the CCP during the Yenan period. The excerpts, quoted below, from a lecture he delivered at the Institute of Marxism-Leninism in Yenan in 1939, give us Liu's ideas on the qualities a dedicated Communist needs to possess. The reading is taken from the English version published by Peking in 1964. Whereas Mao emphasizes the subordination of the party members' personal interests to the interests of the masses, in whom Mao had such great faith, it is noteworthy that Liu demands absolute loyalty to the party.

Personal interests must be subordinated to the Party's interests, the interests of the local Party organization to those of the entire Party, the interests of the part to those of the whole, and temporary to long-term interests. This is a Marxist-Leninist principle which must be followed by every Communist. . . .

From Liu Shao-ch'i, *How to Be a Good Communist* (Peking: Foreign Languages Press, 1964), pp. 45–52.

Comrade Mao Tse-tung once said:

"At no time and in no circumstances should a Communist place his personal interests first; he should subordinate them to the interests of the nation and of the masses of the people. Hence, selfishness, slacking, corruption, striving for the limelight, etc. are most contemptible, while selflessness, working with all one's energy, whole-hearted devotion to public duty, and quiet hard work are the qualities that command respect."

The test of a Party member's loyalty to the Party, the revolution and the cause of communism is whether or not he can subordinate his personal interests absolutely and unconditionally to the interests of the Party, whatever the circumstances. . . .

If a Party member thinks only of the communist interests and aims of the Party, is really selfless and has no personal aims and considerations divorced from those of the Party, and if he ceaselessly raises the level of his political consciousness through revolutionary practice and through the study of Marxism-Leninism, then the following ensues.

First, he has a high communist morality. Taking a clear-cut, firm proletarian stand, he is able to show loyalty to and love for all comrades, all revolutionaries and working people, help them unreservedly and act towards them as his equals, and he will never allow himself to hurt a single one of them for his own interests. He is able to feel for others, place himself in their position, and be considerate of them. On the other hand, he is able to wage resolute struggle against the pernicious enemies of mankind and persevere in the fight for the interests of the Party, the proletariat, and the emancipation of the nation and all mankind. He is "the first to worry and the last to enjoy himself." Whether in the Party or among the people, he is the first to suffer hardship and the last to enjoy comfort; he compares himself with others not with respect to material enjoyment but to the amount of work done for the revolution and the spirit of hard endurance in struggle. In times of adversity he steps forward boldly, and in times of difficulty he does his duty to the full. He has such revolutionary firmness and integrity that "neither riches nor honours can corrupt him, neither poverty nor lowly condition can make him swerve from principle, neither threats nor force can bend him."

Second, he has the greatest revolutionary courage. Having no selfish motives, he has nothing to fear. Having done nothing to give himself a guilty conscience, he can only bare and courageously correct his mistakes and shortcomings, which are like "an eclipse of the sun or the moon" [clearly evident for all men to see.] Because he has the courage of righteous conviction, he never fears the truth, courageously upholds it, spreads it and fights for it. Even if it is temporarily to his disadvantage and if, in upholding the truth, he suffers blows of all kinds, is opposed or censured by most other people and so finds himself in temporary (and honourable) isolation, even to the point where he may have to give up his life, he will still breast the waves to uphold the truth and will never drift with the tide.

Third, he learns how best to grasp the theory and method of Marxism-Leninism. He is able to apply them in keenly observing problems and in knowing and changing reality. Because he takes a clear-cut, firm proletarian stand and is tempered in Marxism-Leninism, he is free from personal apprehensions and self-interest, so that there is no impediment to his observation of things or distortion of his understanding of the truth. He seeks the truth from the facts, and he tests all theories and distinguishes what is true from what is false in revolutionary practice. He does not take a dogmatist or empiricist approach to Marxism-Leninism but integrates the universal truth of Marxism-Leninism with concrete revolutionary practice.

Fourth, he is the most sincere, most candid and happiest of men. Because he has no private axe to grind, nothing to conceal from the Party, and nothing he cannot tell others, he has no problems of personal gain or loss and no personal anxieties other than for the interests of the Party and the revolution. Even when he is working on his own without supervision and is therefore in a position to do something bad, he is just as "watchful over himself when he is alone" and does not do anything harmful. His work bears examination and he is not afraid of having it checked. He does not fear criticism and at the same time is able to criticize others with courage and sincerity.

Fifth, he has the greatest self-respect and self-esteem. For the sake of the Party and the revolution he can be most forbearing and tolerant towards comrades and can suffer wrong in the general interest, even enduring misunderstanding and humiliation without bitterness if the occasion so demands. No personal aims lead him to flatter anyone or to desire flattery from others. When it comes to personal matters, he knows how to conduct himself and has no need to humble himself in order to get help from others. He knows how to take good care of himself in the interests of the Party and the revolution and how to strengthen both his grasp of theory and his practical effectiveness. But when it is necessary to swallow humiliation and bear a heavy load for some important purpose in the cause of the Party and the revolution, he can take on the most difficult and vital tasks without the slightest reluctance, never passing the difficulties to others.

A member of the Communist Party should possess the finest and highest human virtues and take a clear-cut and firm Party and proletarian stand (that is, possess Party spirit and class spirit). Ours is a fine morality precisely because it is proletarian and communist. It is founded not on the protection of the interests of individuals or of the exploiting few, but on those of the proletariat and the great mass of working people, of the cause of the final emancipation of all mankind, the liberation of the whole world from the calamities of capitalism, and the building of a happy and beautiful communist world—it is a morality founded on the Marxist-Leninist theory of scientific communism. As we Communists see it, nothing can be more worthless or indefensible than to sacrifice oneself in the interests of an individual or a small minority. But it is the worthiest and justest thing in the world to sacrifice oneself for the Party, for the proletariat, for the emancipation of the nation and of all mankind, for social progress and for the highest interests of the overwhelming majority of the people. Indeed, countless members of the Communist Party have looked death calmly in the face and made the ultimate sacrifice without the slightest hesitation. Most Communists consider it a matter of courage to die for the sake of the cause, to lay down their life for justice, when that is necessary. This does not stem from any revolutionary fanaticism or hunger for fame but from their scientific understanding of social development and their deep political consciousness. There is no morality in class society to compare with this high communist morality. The universal morality which supposedly transcends class is sheer deceptive nonsense and is in fact a morality designed to protect the interests of the exploiting few. Such a concept of morality is always idealist. It is only we Communists who build our morality on the scientific basis of historical materialism and publicly proclaim its purpose to be the protection of the interests of the proletariat in the struggle for the emancipation of itself and of all mankind.

HUNG-MAO TIEN*

An Appraisal of the Kuomintang's Nanking Decade

Professor Tien discusses the Kuomintang power structure and its nation-building activities during the decade preceding the war with Japan, and analyzes the nature of the weaknesses which undermined the Nationalist government.

There has been a good deal of speculation on whether or not the 1949 Communist victory in China was inevitable. Proponents of one thesis have argued that social and political change there in the first half of the twentieth century made a profound social revolution necessary and inevitable. According to them China was such a sick society that no marginal change would have been sufficient to save her. Their equally vociferous opponents attribute the Communist success to the outbreak of the Sino-Japanese War and the inept postwar China policy of the United States. They maintain that the Kuomintang would have been able to defeat the Communists and unite China had the war not intervened.

To students of modern China these arguments have become familiar themes. Although both serve to emphasize particular aspects of modern China's social and political history, the controversy remains unsettled in the eyes of this writer. Indeed, we still know very little about China in the 1920's and the 1930's; even many aspects of the war and the postwar period remain unclear. . . .

The Kuomintang, which under various names had been politically active for over a quarter of a century, emerged in 1927 as the leading political force in China. It came to power in a period of political decay. The imperial order had been destroyed, and a decentralized warlord

Reprinted from pp. 177–182 of *Government and Politics in Kuomintang China 1927–1937* by Hung-Mao Tien with the permission of the publishers, Stanford University Press © 1972 by the Board of Trustees of the Leland Stanford Junior University.

*Hung-Mao Tien is Associate Professor of Political Science at the University of Wisconsin, Waukesha.

system had grown up to replace it. The feudalization of political power and the breakdown of the centralized bureaucracy posed serious problems for the Kuomintang. The consolidation of this power and of fragmented territorial units became the most crucial task in the struggle to build a nation.

Like many modern nationalist political parties in the Afro-Asian world, the Kuomintang considered itself the only legitimate party and the only party capable of leading efforts toward national integration. The available evidence, however, indicates the party's clear limitations in developing institutional mechanisms to achieve this goal. Especially telling is its failure to build a membership and an organizational structure outside Kwangtung, its initial sanctuary, and the provinces of the middle and lower Yangtze valley. Moreover, a legitimate decision-making structure was never developed within the party itself. Several institutions initially designed to determine policy gradually evolved into bodies with more political status than power. Appointments to the Central Executive Committee, the Political Council, and their standing committees, for example, were used to reward political supporters of the regime and to appease political opponents. As a result these bodies grew in size and became increasingly ineffective. The failure to develop legitimate decision-making institutions meant that power lay with whoever had the force to back up his political ambitions. Chiang Kai-shek emerged as the man with that force.

The Kuomintang regime dominated by Chiang Kai-shek had three prominent characteristics in the 1927–37 decade. First, the central party and the government became militarized; that is, authority was largely controlled by military men and resources were allocated according to military priorities. This militarization precluded the development of both civilian leadership and an institutional base to support such leadership. It enabled Chiang to buttress his power in a military structure that was largely independent of civilian control by the party or the government. It also enabled him to ignore social, political, and international issues that he preferred not to face.

Second, the regime's authority structure came to be dominated by informal client groups connected with Chiang, namely, the Blue Shirts, the C.C. Clique, and the Political Study Clique. Relations between Chiang and the members of these groups were based on such particularistic factors as school ties and local affinity. Although the client groups consisted of both civilians and military men, civilian members believed in upholding Chiang's military power. The cliques effectively blocked other competing senior civilian leaders from exercising influence in the determination of public policy. Party leaders such as Hu Han-min and Wang Ching-wei, although they had prestige and followers, were fatally handicapped by the lack of stable, independent bases of power. The ·elimination of Hu, Wang, and others from the decision-making process had unfortunate repercussions for the regime, which needed a broad-based consensus on fundamental policies. In part, it tended to perpetuate regionally based power groups, since some civilian leaders who were alienated from the regime made alliances with regional or provincial forces against Nanking. Thus, in the final analysis, although Chiang's ability to replace his rivals with loyal followers may have gained him the dominant position in the regime, it also created factors that threatened to undermine his pursuit of real power.

Finally, under Chiang and his extremely conservative and ultranationalistic client groups, the regime moved in the direction of fascism. There was a growing emphasis on the techniques of political control and on the personification of political power in an infallible leader, Chiang Kai-shek. The activities of the Blue Shirts and the C.C. Clique clearly reflect an attempt to transform the Kuomintang into a party of a fascist nature. Chiang's supporters moved step by step to institute control mechanisms in rural areas within the regime's jurisdiction. The resulting mobilization of some members of the rural population was not intended to incorporate them into the political process in any meaningful way; instead it was part of a concentrated effort to organize a mass following for Chiang. This whole trend toward fascism was ultimately detrimental to the party and to Chiang himself. The Kuomintang had inherited a genuine revolutionary legacy, however incomplete and unsystematic its performance had been in implementing it. The new emphasis on control placed Chiang in the impossible position of affirming revolution and the status quo simultaneously. Furthermore, the party was operating in a sociopolitical environment that had been thoroughly disrupted; few viable systems existed to uphold the status quo. What China truly needed was drastic change, neither control nor maintenance of the existing order. This does not mean that the success of the Communists was inevitable. The Kuomintang had a chance to promote major changes short of revolution. Perhaps if other, more progressive, party leaders had had more power, they would have done so.

The changes and developments in the Kuomintang's power structure shaped the patterns of the party's nation-building. In 1927 China was still plagued by regional militarism. By 1935–36 the regime had extended its political influence from the two provinces that it initially controlled, Chekiang and Kiangsu, to eight other provinces: Anhwei, Kiangsi, Hupeh, Honan, Hunan, Fukien, and, to a lesser degree, Kansu and Shensi. Much of this central penetration was made possible by anti-Communist military operations. Communist activities in these provinces posed a serious threat to local rulers, who could not suppress them alone. Since Chiang Kai-shek was committed to eliminating the Communists, he was able to force his way into certain areas on the basis of this common interest. Most provincial rulers who had to deal with the Communists came to accept some degree of central authority, as exercised by Chiang's military headquarters. Chiang adopted the same strategy of central penetration in Szechwan and Kweichow in 1935–36, but the outbreak of the Sino-Japanese War in 1937 cut short these attempts.

The important questions concerning the provinces are to what extent was the Kuomintang able to effect changes there and by what means did it do so. In summary, we may draw the following conclusions regarding relations between the center and the provinces and the political developments that resulted from this interaction. First, by the end of the decade the Kuomintang had established political authority, in varying degrees, in the ten provinces classified as the Bandit Suppression Zones. It was able to introduce certain administrative changes in these provinces and to influence the selection of provincial and county-level administrative personnel. The Kuomintang authority was not free, however, to make appointments without consulting provincial rulers. In fact, compromises were often necessary to avoid provoking serious opposition. Neither was Nanking able to establish a uniform, centralized administrative system throughout the zones. Matters of provincial finance continued to remain outside central control. In short, Chiang Kai-shek and the Kuomintang regime were forced to rely on political bargaining and compromise to achieve their ends.

Second, the major instrument of central penetration was the Military Council, which was headed by Chiang Kai-shek and had field headquarters in Nanchang and later in Wuchang and Chungking. These headquarters, not party or government bodies, exercised political control in the Bandit Suppression Provinces. Nanking's resources were allocated largely by the military headquarters for purposes determined by Chiang and his followers. The limited changes effected in the provinces by the center were also closely related to military objectives. The regime's major agents were military men and members of Chiang's client factions, whose selection and activities were largely outside the control of Nanking's civilian authorities. Thus there was little chance that central penetration would result in the development of strong provincial administrative and party institutions.

Third, little was accomplished in the way of socioeconomic reform. The central government and all provincial governments continued to allocate most of their resources to military, quasi-military, and administrative purposes. The percentage of revenues allocated to improving socioeconomic conditions was relatively small. This no doubt was responsible for further socioeconomic decline, particularly in rural China. Both central and provincial authorities, although they needed much larger incomes, were slow to improve mechanisms of taxation. The financial reforms sponsored by Nanking did bring some minor improvements, but the traditional taxation system continued to prevail in most places, growing more corrupt and inequitable. This was symptomatic of a general disintegration of socioeconomic systems in most of China outside the major cities and walled towns.

Finally, outside the ten Bandit Suppression Provinces, the Kuomintang's authority was nominal or nonexistent. A high degree of provincialism continued to exist in Shansi, Kwangsi, Kwangtung, Yunnan, and Szechwan. Varying degrees of autonomy also existed in Kweichow and the outlying provinces in the north and northwest. Here provincial or regional militarists appointed their own officials and ran their own administrative and financial affairs with little or no concern for the wishes of the central authority. On the one hand, we may speculate that even if the Communists had not been active and there had been no war with Japan, it would have taken the Kuomintang a long time to bring these provinces into its domain. On the other hand, we are assessing the Kuomintang's performance over a relatively short period of ten years. This performance may compare favorably with that of many developing nations after World War II.

Still, it does not necessarily follow that if there had been enough time, the Kuomintang under Chiang Kai-shek would have managed to build an integrated nation. In fact, the evidence presented here tends to argue against that.

JOHN S. SERVICE*

The Disintegration of the KMT Government

After the Sino-Japanese War broke out in 1937, the bankruptcy of the KMT policies became increasingly evident and the government lost its power of leadership. The following extracts from a memorandum written by Mr. Service in 1944, when he was a United States Foreign Service Officer in China, provide a highly perceptive assessment of the situation under the Nationalist government.

China faces economic collapse. This is causing disintegration of the army and the government's administrative apparatus. It is one of the chief causes of growing political unrest. The Generalissimo is losing the support of a China which, by unity in the face of violent aggression, found a new and unexpected strength during the first two years of the war with Japan. Internal weaknesses are becoming accentuated and there is taking place a reversal of the process of unification.

1. Morale is low and discouragement widespread. There is a general feeling of hopelessness.

2. The authority of the Central Government is weakening in the areas away from the larger cities. Government mandates and measures of control cannot be enforced and remain ineffective. It is becoming difficult for the Government to collect enough food for its huge army and bureaucracy.

3. The governmental and military structure is being permeated and demoralized from top to bottom by corruption, unprecedented in scale and openness.

4. The intellectual and salaried classes, who have suffered the most heavily from inflation, are in danger of liquidation. The academic

From *The China White Paper: August 1949* [originally issued as *United States Relations with China: With Special Reference to the Period 1944–1949;* Department of State Publications 3573, Far Eastern Series 30] (Stanford: Stanford University Press, 1967), pp. 567–569.

*John S. Service served in China from 1933 to 1945 as an Officer of the U.S. State Department. He is currently on the staff of the Center for Chinese Studies at the University of California, Berkeley.

groups suffer not only the attrition and demoralization of economic stress; the weight of years of political control and repression is robbing them of the intellectual vigor and leadership they once had.

5. Peasant resentment of the abuses of conscription, tax collection and other arbitrary impositions has been widespread and is growing. The danger is ever-increasing that past sporadic outbreaks of banditry and agrarian unrest may increase in scale and find political motivation.

6. The provincial groups are making common cause with one another and with other dissident groups, and are actively consolidating their positions. Their continuing strength in the face of the growing weakness of the Central Government is forcing new measures of political appeasement in their favor.

7. Unrest within the Kuomintang armies is increasing, as shown in one important instance by the 'Young Generals conspiracy' late in 1943. On a higher plane, the war zone commanders are building up their own spheres of influence and are thus creating a 'new warlordism.'

•   •   •

9. The Kuomintang is losing the respect and support of the people by its selfish policies and its refusal to heed progressive criticism. It seems unable to revivify itself with fresh blood, and its unchanging leadership shows a growing ossification and loss of a sense of reality. To combat the dissensions and cliquism within the Party, which grows more rather than less acute, the leadership is turning toward the reactionary and unpopular Chen brothers clique.

10. The Generalissimo shows a similar loss of realistic flexibility and a hardening of narrowly conservative views. His growing megalomania and his unfortunate attempts to be 'sage' as well as leader—shown, for instance, by 'China's Destiny' and his book on economics—have forfeited the respect of many intellectuals, who enjoy in China a position of unique influence. Criticism of his dictatorship is becoming outspoken. . . .

The Kuomintang shows no intention of relaxing the authoritarian controls on which its present power depends. Far from discarding or reducing the paraphernalia of a police state—the multiple and omnipresent secret police organizations, the Gendarmerie, and so forth—it continues to strengthen them as its last resort for internal security.

ON THE ECONOMIC FRONT

•   •   •

It is directly responsible for the increase of official corruption which is one of the main obstacles to any rational attempt to ameliorate the financial situation. It does nothing to stop large-scale profiteering, hoarding and speculation—all of which are carried on by people either powerful in the Party or with intimate political connections.

It fails to carry out effective mobilization of resources. Such measures of war-time control as it has promulgated have remained a dead letter or have intensified the problems they were supposedly designed to remedy—as for instance ill-advised and poorly executed attempts at price regulation.

It passively allows both industrial and the more important handicraft production to run down, as they of course must when it is more profitable for speculators to hold raw materials than to have them go through the normal productive process.

It fails to carry out rationing except in a very limited way, or to regulate the manufacture and trade of luxury goods, many of which come from areas under Japanese control. It shows little concern that these imports are largely paid for with strategic commodities of value to the enemy.

It fails to make an effective attempt to reduce the budgetary deficit and increase revenue by tapping such resources as excess profits and incomes of landlords and merchants. It allows its tax-collecting apparatus to bog down in corruption and inefficiency—to the point that possibly not more than one-third of revenues collected reach the government. It continues to spend huge government funds on an idle and useless Party bureaucracy.

At best, it passively watches inflation gather momentum without even attempting palliative measures available to it, such as the aggressive sale of gold and foreign currency.

It refuses to attack the fundamental economic problems of China such as the growing concentration of land holdings, extortionate rents and ruinous interest rates, and the impact of inflation. . . .

MAURICE MEISNER*

Maoism and the Success of the Communist Party

The ultimate success of the CCP came from the way it utilized the situation created by the Japanese invasion to mobilize the peasantry and win it over to the Communist cause. Professor Meisner analyzes the nature of the mass nationalism and its correlation to Maoism, the ideology developed by Mao Tse-tung by a "creative interpretation" of Marxism and Leninism.

THE YENAN ERA AND PEASANT REVOLUTION

If the Communist military position in 1936 was precarious at best, the social and economic environment in which they now found themselves was hardly any more promising. Northern Shensi was one of the poorest and most backward areas of modern China. Centuries of erosion of its loess topsoil had made its lands barren and infertile, capable of supporting only a relatively small and extremely impoverished population —"a very poor, backward, underdeveloped, and mountainous part of the country," as Mao Tse-tung once remarked to a foreign visitor who had toured the province.[1] And, to Chou En-lai in 1936, it seemed a most inauspicious place to revive the revolution. He complained:

> Peasants in Shensi are extremely poor, their land very unproductive. . . . The population of the Kiangsi Soviet numbered 3,000,000 whereas here it is at most 600,000. . . . In Kiangsi and Fukien people brought bundles with them when they joined the Red Army; here they do not even bring chopsticks; they are utterly destitute.[2]

And what of Yenan itself, the most sacred city to which pilgrimages are made to view the historic revolutionary places, especially the austere wooden houses and cave dwellings where Mao and others lived

From pp. 275–288 of "Yenan Communism and the Rise of the Chinese Republic" by Maurice Meisner, in *Modern East Asia: Essays in Interpretation,* edited by James B. Crowley, © 1970 by Harcourt Brace Jovanovich, Inc., and reprinted with their permission.

*Professor Maurice Meisner, Fellow of the Center for Advanced Study in the Behavioral Sciences at Stanford, California, 1966–1967, is teaching history at the University of Wisconsin.

and worked during that legendary decade? Although an ancient city, founded some three thousand years ago, it cannot claim a particularly distinguished history. As Chinese civilization moved southward over the centuries, Yenan became a remote and unknown frontier town, used mostly as an advanced military outpost to defend the northern borders against nomadic invaders from central Asia. It was little more than a dreary and impoverished market town of perhaps ten thousand people when it was occupied by Communist troops at the end of 1936 and established as the administrative capital of what was to be called the Shensi-Kansu-Ningsia Border Region. The wretched poverty of the entire area in which the Communists now operated was reflected in the bleakness of Yenan. The town's famous museums and shrines exhibit no ancient, historic glories but are products of modern revolutionary history—and, in a sense, are the result of an accident of history. ("We didn't pick it" was Mao's terse reply to a sympathetic American writer who once politely praised Yenan's harsh climate.)[3]

But it is Yenan the time, not Yenan the place, that Chinese Communists celebrate. Yet how did the time become one to celebrate when the place was so unfavorable? How did a force of thirty thousand revolutionaries, isolated in an area so remote and so lacking in economic and material resources, grow within a decade into a powerful army of more than a million men and acquire the massive peasant support upon which its momentous and overwhelming victory was to be based?

Little light is shed on these questions by pondering that most quoted of Maoist maxims: "Political power grows out of the barrel of a gun." To be sure, an important modern Chinese political reality is reflected in this slogan: The disintegration of traditional Chinese forms of political authority and sources of legitimacy had produced a twentieth-century historical situation in which the effective exercise of political power was in fact largely dependent on the control of effective military force. But Mao Tse-tung was not the first to discover this particular secret of modern Chinese political life. Chiang K'ai-shek, for one, had learned the lesson earlier, and it was, in fact, Chiang's control of an effective army in 1927 that was mainly responsible for the Communist disasters of that year. Moreover, "political power grows out of the barrel of a gun" is hardly a formula for political victory, even if it is a more or less accurate description of the character of modern Chinese politics. Still less is it an explanation for the victory prepared during the Yenan decade. For the fact remains that in 1936 the Communists in Shensi had few guns (even fewer guns than men to hold them), and they possessed what guns they had in an environment where the economic and human resources necessary for the development of military power were severely limited. It is, in short, necessary to explain how they acquired guns—and the men willing to use them—in order to understand how Communist political power did in fact grow in China.

We shall turn shortly to the many internal prerequisites for the Communist military and political success. But first it is necessary to take note of a crucial external factor—the Japanese invasion and its effects—that transformed the Chinese political scene and redefined the internal prerequisites for revolutionary victory.

For those inclined to ponder the role of "accidents" in history, the Japanese invasion of China is undoubtedly a most intriguing case. Were it not for the Japanese attempt to conquer China in 1937, it can plausibly be argued, the conditions essential to the Communist victory would not have been present. Yenan would have remained an obscure and unheralded market town in a remote Chinese province, unknown to Chinese and foreigners alike. No one in Peking today would be celebrating "the Yenan spirit," and no "China watchers" would be deliberating the implications of "the Yenan syndrome." The whole course of recent Chinese history—and indeed of world history—would probably have been profoundly different.

Those who are inclined to seek universal patterns of historical development can find in the Japanese invasion of China a classic case of one of the oldest and most persistent of historical patterns: the intimate relationship between war and revolution. For students of communism, it is of special interest to note that all *indigenous* communist revolutions (with one dubious exception[4]) grew out of conditions created by major wars; more precisely, they grew as war and foreign invasion undermined the power and authority of existing socio-political orders. The Russian October Revolution of 1917 was in large measure the product of conditions created in Russian society by World War I. And it was the foreign invasions of World War II that produced the conditions for successful communist revolutions in Yugoslavia and Vietnam as well as in China.

However intriguing it might be to pursue the question of the relationship between war and revolution (and this is a matter that deserves the most serious consideration), there is little to be gained from viewing the Communist revolution in China solely in terms of some inevitable and universally valid model of this relationship. For the

Communist success, as we shall have occasion to observe, was by no means the inevitable historical result of the Japanese invasion.

Nor can we interpret the Japanese invasion itself—as its results—as simply an "accident" of history. There were compelling political, economic, and ideological forces—as well as a variety of factors operating in the realm of international diplomacy—that led to the Japanese decision to attempt to conquer China. And that decision was not uninfluenced by the Chinese historical situation—or, more precisely, by Japanese perceptions of the weakness of China. Yet, if the invasion was not a historical accident, it was to China an external event, in the sense that it was determined by forces over which Chinese had little or no control. Neither the Nationalists (who lost a good deal of their credentials as Chinese nationalists by their feeble responses to the Japanese threat) nor the Communists (who gained considerable political capital by their consistent advocacy of national resistance to the foreign invaders) could decisively influence the course of Japanese policy in China.

It is not likely to prove fruitful to speculate about what might or might not have happened had circumstances been different; but it is important to understand just what did happen in the existing circumstances. As we have just suggested, these circumstances—the Japanese occupation and its effects on Chinese society—proved highly favorable to the realization of Communist ends. For one thing, the Japanese undermined the foundations of the Kuomintang regime, for the Nationalists were driven from the major cities, which were their primary sources of financial and political support. For the Kuomintang, the ravages of war resulted in incredible economic chaos and bureaucratic corruption—and, eventually, in almost total demoralization. More importantly, such administrative authority as the Kuomintang had managed to exercise in the countryside was largely destroyed, and members of the gentry-landlord class, upon which that fragile authority had rested, either fled the rural areas or were left militarily and politically defenseless. At the same time, the Communists, already experienced in working in the villages among the peasantry and adept at guerrilla warfare, were given access to vast areas of the countryside. For, while the Japanese invaders were able to occupy the cities, where the Kuomintang had been based, they did not have the manpower to effectively control the countryside, where Communist guerrilla bases multiplied rapidly during the war years. The retreat of Kuomintang military forces to the west in the face of invading Japanese armies, and the concurrent collapse of Nationalist governmental authority in much of China, allowed the Communists to break out of their remote sanctuary in Shensi and expand their military and political influence through vast areas of the countryside in northern and central China. Although the increasingly powerful Yenan base area remained the political and ideological center of the Communist revolution, Communist cadres operated in many parts of rural China, gaining the political support of tens of millions of peasants and organizing many for guerrilla warfare behind Japanese lines. Some Communist organizers filtered southward from Shensi, others were survivors from earlier guerrilla bases in central China, and many more were new adherents to the Communist cause. The gradual growth of peasant-supported Communist political and military nuclei in many parts of China during the war years was to prove decisive when the revolutionary struggle with the Kuomintang was resumed with full fury in 1946 in a massive civil war.

Much of the enormous popular support the Communists gained during the war years was based on patriotic appeals for national resistance to the foreign invaders. The new banner of modern Chinese nationalism had replaced the old "Mandate of Heaven" as the symbol of political legitimacy in twentieth-century China. As that banner began to slip from old Kuomintang hands in the 1930's—at first because of their seeming unwillingness to defend the nation against the Japanese threat and then because of their obvious inability to do so—it was quickly picked up and eagerly hoisted by new Communist hands. During the war years, Yenan was not only the revolutionary center but also (for increasing numbers of Chinese) the symbol of Chinese nationalist resistance to the Japanese. From the cities many thousands of students and intellectuals migrated to Yenan to join the Communist (and now also the nationalist) cause—and there, at the Northwest Anti-Japanese Red Army University, many were trained (and also "ideologically remolded") to become important political, administrative, and military cadres for the rapidly expanding Communist base and guerrilla areas. Of far greater political importance was the Communists' ability to organize the peasantry on the basis of patriotic as well as socio-economic appeals. The Japanese occupation not only intensified the economic crisis in the countryside but gave rise to the most bitter antiforeign sentiments among the peasants. These the Communists were able to transform into a modern mass nationalist movement and utilize for revolutionary political ends. This new Communist political opportunity was greatly facilitated by the ruthless policies pursued by the

Japanese invaders—the brutal and indiscriminate military forays into the villages of northern and central China, which Japanese soldiers could plunder and punish but could not hold and occupy. Indeed, in the areas to which the Communists were able to gain access, the mobilization of the peasant masses on the basis of an anti-Japanese nationalist program contributed enormously to the military and political successes of the Yenan period.

In view of the strong tendency to interpret Chinese Communism as a species of Chinese nationalism or to view the Communist revolution as a case of a new elite riding to power on a fortuitous wave of mass nationalism, it is important to keep the whole phenomenon of "peasant nationalism" in proper historical perspective. For one thing, the Chinese peasants' sense of identification with China as a political entity and resistance to foreign intruders and invaders are not phenomena that suddenly appeared on the Chinese scene in 1937; both are age-old features of Chinese history. Even armed peasant resistance to modern imperialist incursions has a rich, almost century-old history prior to the Japanese invasion, beginning with the Opium War of 1839–42. Second, it would be highly misleading either to overestimate the spontaneous origins of the peasantry's precisely modern sense of "national consciousness" or to underestimate the role of Communist cadres in instilling that modern sense of nationalism in the strategy of "people's war." The Communists did not suddenly become nationalists during the war because they had become immersed in a nationalistic rural environment; they were ardent nationalists long before 1937, and they played a crucial role (through both propaganda and organization) in transforming the elemental antiforeign response of the peasantry into a truly modern nationalist response. By forging bonds of solidarity among peasants from various localities and regions, the Communists created a nationwide movement of resistance and imbued it with a sense of national mission that otherwise would have been absent. The Chinese Communists, in large measure, brought Chinese nationalism to the countryside; they did not simply reflect it.

Furthermore, however important Communist nationalist appeals were in gaining mass peasant support, socio-economic issues were at least equally important. The war intensified the already horrendous economic burdens of the peasantry and thus increased the attractiveness of the Communist program for land reform. To be sure, the official land policy of the Yenan period was a relatively moderate one by Kiangsi standards. Instead of the outright expropriation and division of landlord holdings, the Communists adopted a program for reductions in rents and interest rates, partly to conform to the terms of the tenuous wartime alliance with the Kuomintang but more importantly as an attempt to enlist the support of landlords and "rich peasants," as well as the masses of poor peasants, in the struggle against the Japanese occupation. But the reduction of rent to no more than one-third of the crop and the elimination of the many extralegal means through which landlords and bureaucrats traditionally exploited peasants in China were hardly unappealing measures to those who had been subjected to the most merciless forms of economic, as well as social and political, oppression.

Moreover, the officially "moderate" agrarian policies were by no means universally followed. In many cases large landholdings were in fact expropriated and distributed among land-hungry peasants, especially in areas where landlords fled with retreating Kuomintang armies. Where the gentry-landlord elite remained, collaboration between Chinese landlords and Japanese occupiers was not uncommon; in exchange for political services performed—which is to say, the traditional gentry function of "social control"—the Japanese allowed the gentry their traditional economic privilege of exploiting the peasantry. In such cases, the traditional hatred of the landlord for socio-economic reasons was intensified by new, nationalist resentments, and the Communists appealed to both feelings simultaneously, promoting class as well as national struggle. The fact of the matter, then, is that expropriation and division of gentry landholdings was a highly popular policy in much of the countryside; and where it occurred, the Communist party—if it had sufficient military predominance to guarantee the security of the peasants and their newly acquired land—won over masses of loyal peasant followers.

The view that the Communists acquired their massive peasant support in the Yenan period by a combination of nationalist appeals and moderate land policies that did not radically change existing social relationships is simply not tenable. Conditions and policies of course varied greatly from area to area. In some areas, social revolutionary actions were sacrificed to obtain the support of all rural classes in the interests of national unity; in others, radical land policies proved more effective in gaining peasant support than purely nationalist appeals; and, in still other areas, neither nationalist nor socio-economic appeals were effective. But, even where the officially moderate land policies were pursued, traditional agrarian relationships were profoundly transformed: The local political power of the gentry elite was broken, its social authority and prestige were gravely undermined, and such reduced economic power as it still held was dependent on the grace of the new holders of political and military power in the local areas—the cadres of the Chinese Communist party. In the areas under Communist control in the Yenan era, the undermining and sometimes the destruction of the power of the gentry-landlord class—the ruling elite of Chinese society for two thousand years—marked the beginning of a social revolution that was to culminate in the late 1940's and early 1950's in the elimination of the gentry as a social class throughout China. It was to be the first genuine social revolution in Chinese history since the establishment of the imperial order in 221 B.C.

Thus the Japanese invasion, by removing the Kuomintang armies and bureaucracies from vast areas of China and by undermining the power and prestige of traditional power-holders and elite groups (warlords and gentry), created conditions highly favorable to the Communists—and perhaps ones that were crucial to the eventual Communist victory. The invasion did not in itself create a revolutionary situation (for that already existed), but it did much to intensify and aggravate conditions conducive to revolution and to provide new opportunities for revolutionary action. But "revolutionary situations," however mature, do not in themselves create revolutions. Only men make revolutions—and only on the basis of their consciousness, their perception of the situation in which they find themselves, and their will and ability to transform that situation in accordance with their revolutionary goals. The war, in short, by no means guaranteed the inevitability of a Communist victory. And the successes and specific characteristics of Yenan Communism did not spring spontaneously from any "objective" imperatives of the wartime situation. Rather, they owed much to the way in which the Chinese Communists perceived the Chinese historical situation and to the way in which they were disposed to go about changing it. Thus, to understand the Yenan era and its distinctive revolutionary and ideological legacy, it is necessary to take into account subjective as well as objective factors, particularly the intellectual and ideological predispositions of Mao Tse-tung.

THE ORIGINS OF MAOISM

Although "Maoism" did not crystalize into an official ideological orthodoxy until the Yenan period, its historical existence as a distinct (and distinctively Chinese) interpretation of Marxism began with the introduction of Marxism in China in 1918–19. To view Maoism as simply the ideological product or reflection of the "objective" conditions of Yenan Communism is to ignore the historical truism that men are the producers as well as the products of history, and that the way in which they make history depends, at least in part, on the way they perceive objective reality. Neither Yenan Communism nor Mao Tse-tung are exceptions to this proposition; much of what went into the making of the former was molded by the now famous "thoughts" of the latter. And Mao did not arrive in Shensi in 1935 with an empty head.

In fact, when Mao became a convert to Marxism and communism in 1919, the basic intellectual predispositions that were to mold his understanding and interpretation of Marxism and his concept of revolution were already present, and they were to be reinforced by his revolutionary experiences in the 1920's and early 1930's. While it is well beyond the scope of this essay to trace the intellectual development of Mao Tse-tung, it is possible to identify certain abiding traits of the Maoist mentality that provided the essential intellectual and ideological prerequisites for the successful Yenan strategy of revolution.

By no means the least important of Mao's early (and persisting) intellectual orientations was a profoundly voluntarist belief that the decisive factor in history is human consciousness—the ideas, the wills, and the actions of men. This faith in the ability of self-conscious men to mold objective social reality in accordance with their ideas and ideals survived the influence of the more deterministic tenets of Marxist theory, as Mao began to assimilate that theory in the 1920's and 1930's.

The survival of this fundamental voluntarist impulse, it might be noted, was greatly facilitated by the manner in which Marxism had come to China in the wake of World War I. Unlike Russia and the Western countries, China lacked a Marxist social-democratic tradition. The early Chinese converts to communism were drawn to Marxism and Leninism by the chiliastic message of the Russian Bolshevik revolution (which promised both national liberation and worldwide revolution) and were committed to a Leninist-style revolution long before they became familiar with Marxist-Leninist theory. These early communists (such as Li Ta-chao, China's first Marxist, and his disciple, Mao Tse-tung) tended to interpret Marxist theory in the light of their revolutionary expectations rather than to redefine those expectations on the basis of their new Marxist creed.

To be sure, Mao derived from the objective laws of historical development proclaimed by Marx some degree of assurance in the historical inevitability of a socialist future (and he soon learned to repeat the relevant Marxist formulas). But, in the final analysis, his faith in the achievement of that future was not based upon any real Marxist confidence in the determining, objective forces of socio-historical development; it stemmed rather from a profound confidence in the revolutionary consciousness and activism of men determined to bring about that future. For Mao, in other words, the essential factor in determining the course of history was conscious human activity, and the most important ingredients for revolution were the attitudes of men and their willingness to engage in revolutionary action.

This implied, among other things, that revolution in China need not be dependent on any predetermined levels of social and economic development and that immediate opportunities for revolutionary action need not be restricted by orthodox Marxist-Leninist formulas. It also implied a special concern for developing and maintaining "correct" ideological consciousness, the ulitmately decisive factor in determining revolutionary success or failure. Correct thought, in the Maoist view, is the first and essential prerequisite for correct revolutionary action, and it is this assumption that lies behind the emphasis on the peculiarly Chinese Communist techniques of "thought reform" and "ideological remolding" developed and refined in the Yenan period. The Cheng Feng campaign of 1942–44 for the rectification of "undesirable" ideas and ideological tendencies was the most intensive application of a general Chinese Communist policy.

This whole emphasis on ideological solidarity was of central importance to the successful conduct of guerrilla warfare in the Yenan period. In a "guerrilla" situation, where centralized forms of organizational control are by definition precluded, the forging of the strongest possible commitments to a common ideology and a common manner of thinking (and thus of acting) becomes a matter of supreme importance. The fact that Maoism was already disposed to stress the importance of "subjective factors" goes a long way toward explaining why the Communists adopted the strategy of guerrilla warfare and why they were able to employ this strategy so successfully.

If Mao's voluntarism mitigated the more deterministic implications of Marxist theory, his particularly powerful nationalistic proclivities were equally important in making Marxism a more flexible ideological instrument for revolution in China. As was generally true for Chinese intellectuals who were attracted to communism and Marxism in the May

Fourth period, nationalist resentments against Western imperialism and nationalist aspirations for a future "new China" were very much involved in Mao's original conversation to Marxism. Quite apart from the nationalist appeals of the Leninist theory of imperialism and specific Soviet appeals to Chinese nationalist sentiments (both of which promised China an important place in the world revolutionary process), Marxist theory itself satisfied profoundly important nationalist needs. For Mao, as for others, Marxism appeared to be the most advanced product of modern Western thought; but, unlike other Western ideologies and models, it rejected the West in its present capitalist and imperialist form (and thus also rejected the present Western imperialist impingement on China). At the same time, Marxism served to reaffirm the rejection of the already discarded "prenationalist" values of traditional China, which now could be conveniently dismissed as "feudal." In other words, Marxism had the great nationalist appeal of assigning both "precapitalist" China and the capitalist West to the same "dustbin of history" while simultaneously looking toward a "postcapitalist" future in which China would take its rightful place in a new international socialist order.

It goes without saying that Mao has always had a certain feeling of national pride in the Chinese past and that he has been at least as much concerned with the future power and glory of the Chinese nation as with the fate of the international proletarian revolution. But it might also be said that from the beginning Mao's especially deep-rooted nationalist impulses gave rise to the belief that the Chinese revolution was more or less synonymous with the world revolution—or at least that China had a very special, indeed almost messianic, role to play in the world revolutionary process. As early as 1930 Mao felt sufficiently confident to proclaim publicly that China was more revolutionary than other countries and to predict that "the revolution will certainly move towards an upsurge more quickly in China than in Western Europe."[5] In the Maoist conception of China's special place in the world revolution, genuinely internationalist aspirations and goals were no doubt inextricably intertwined with Chinese nationalist impulses. But it was in this treacherous area of "messianic revolutionary nationalism" (as Trotsky once called it) that Mao departed from other Chinese Marxists whose nationalist passions were restrained by more orthodox Western Marxist considerations.

The nationalist element in Mao's Marxist world view was reflected not only in his long-standing hostility to the Russian-dominated Comintern (and, in the late 1950's, in his open hostility toward the Soviet Union) but also, and more importantly, in his conception of revolution within China. Central to this conception was the conviction that the real enemies were not so much within Chinese society as without. The real enemy was foreign imperialism, and in the face of that continuing threat China stood as a potentially proletarian nation in a hostile capitalist-imperialist world order. Although internal class divisions were important and class struggle necessary, in confronting the external foe, it was assumed that Chinese of all social classes could gather under the revolutionary nationalist umbrella held up by the Chinese Communist party—and those who could not, or would not, were excluded from membership in the nation, or at least from "the people," excommunicated as representatives of foreign imperialism. Political circumstances permitting, class struggle thus could be subordinated to national struggle—and, indeed, the two could be regarded as more or less synonymous. In fact, if the main enemy was external, then a "united front" of all Chinese opposed to foreign imperialism was not only necessary for national survival but also conducive to the eventual realization of international communist goals. In Mao's eyes, nationalist struggle was not necessarily incompatible with the pursuit of Marxist internationalist goals.

A third intellectual orientation that decisively influenced the Maoist adaptation of Marxism-Leninism to the Chinese environment may be described as essentially populist. The populist-inspired notion of a "great union of the popular masses"[6] that Mao advocated at the beginning of his revolutionary career in 1919 survived the influence of Marxism and modified the influence of Leninism. Populist impulses reinforced Mao's nationalist-inspired faith in the basic unity of the Chinese people in the face of intrusion by alien forces and led him to attribute to "the people" an almost inherent revolutionary socialist consciousness. "In the masses is embodied great socialist activism" is a recent Maoist slogan that derives from an early Maoist-populist faith, expressed in 1919 in the affirmation that "our Chinese people possesses great intrinsic energy."[7]

Moreover, Mao's populist impulse, with its essentially rural orientation and its romantic celebration of the rural ideal of "the unity of living and working," served to define "the people" as the peasant masses (for the peasantry, after all, constituted the overwhelming majority of the Chinese population) and led him to prize the spontaneously revolutionary energies he believed they possessed. Thus, Mao's populism drew him to the countryside at a time when the Communist revolution was still centered in the cities. In his famous (and heretical) "Hunan Report" of March 1927, he found in the Chinese peasantry an elemental revolutionary force so great that it would sweep away everything before it—including, he predicted, those revolutionary intellectuals who proved unwilling or unable to unite with the peasant masses. Then, as later, he expressed profound distrust of the "knowledge" brought by urban intellectuals and profound admiration for the innate "wisdom" of the peasantry.

Many other characteristic features of the Maoist mentality are typically populist. One might mention, for example, Mao's hostility toward occupational specialization, his acute distrust of intellectuals and specialists, his profoundly antibureaucratic orientations (and indeed his general enmity toward all forms of large-scale, centralized organization), his anti-urban bias, and his romantic mood of heroic revolutionary self-sacrifice. These, as well as many other aspects of the thought of Mao, bear striking similarities to what is generally understood by the term "populism." To be sure, Mao is not simply a populist in Marxist guise (any more than he is simply a Chinese nationalist in communist dress), but it is important to note that populist ideas and impulses have significantly influenced the manner in which Mao has understood and employed Marxism.

To understand the reasons for the Communist success in the Yenan period, it is of special importance to take into account Mao's genuinely populist faith in the peasant masses as potential bearers of socialist revolutionary consciousness. For it is this faith that permitted—and indeed dictated—the much celebrated Maoist notion of "the mass line," the various principles and rules by which Communist cadres became intimately involved and identified with the peasant masses. The Maoist maxim that intellectuals and party cadres must become the pupils of the masses before they can become their teachers was in fact widely practiced in the Yenan days. Had it been otherwise, the Communists could never have acquired the mass support and cooperation among the peasantry that was so essential to the successful employment of the strategy of "people's war."

In attributing a latent socialist consciousness to the peasantry, Mao, it should be noted, departed not only from Marx but from Lenin. For Marx, the bearers of socialist consciousness were the urban proletariat, and he rarely missed an opportunity to express his contempt for "the idiocy of rural life." And for Lenin, socialist consciousness was to be imposed on the "spontaneous" proletarian mass movement by an elite of revolutionary intellectuals organized into a highly centralized and disciplined communist party, with the peasantry playing an ambiguous auxiliary role in the revolutionary process. Mao departed from Leninism not only in his virtually total lack of interest in the urban working class but also in his conception of the nature and role of the party. The party was sacrosanct to Lenin because it was the incarnation of "proletarian consciousness." In his mind, there was no question about who should be the teachers and who the pupils. For Mao, on the other hand, this was precisely the question, and it has remained unanswered; he has never really defined the relationship between the organized "proletarian consciousness" of the party and the spontaneous "proletarian consciousness" of the masses in a purely Leninist fashion. His faith in the party as the bearer of revolutionary consciousness was never complete, for it was accompanied by the populist belief that true revolutionary knowledge and creativity ultimately emanate from the people themselves.

There were, to be sure, objective factors that influenced Mao's rather ambiguous view of the role of the party. Military power, after all, was the crucial factor in determining the outcome of the Chinese revolution, and the influence of the party as such tended to be subsumed by the Red Army. Moreover, unlike the Russian Revolution, the Chinese Communist revolution did not involve the sudden seizure of state power. It was based, rather, on the relatively gradual growth of popular support and, eventually, on the revolutionary activities of millions, often largely spontaneous, that were to take place in many local areas where communication was slow and difficult. This created a revolutionary situation that was hardly conducive to control and direction by a highly centralized party apparatus.

The voluntarist, nationalist, and populist impulses that governed Mao's understanding and interpretation of Marxism in the years after 1919 formed the essential intellectual and ideological prerequisites for the development of the Maoist strategy of peasant revolution and the successful employment of this strategy in the Yenan period. Although the Japanese invasion intensified China's socio-economic crisis and created political conditions favorable to the growth of a revolutionary movement, it was not inevitable that a revolutionary movement would in fact grow and emerge victorious. It is most unlikely that orthodox Marxist-Leninists could have appreciated fully the revolutionary opportunities offered, much less have taken advantage of them to build a communist movement on a purely peasant base. It was precisely Mao's ideological unorthodoxies that allowed the Communists to seize upon these opportunities. It was his voluntarist faith in the power of the human will and consciousness to shape historical reality that permitted him to ignore (or redefine) those Marxist socio-economic prerequisites and Marxist social-class considerations that might otherwise have restricted the possibilities for revolutionary action. It was his nationalist-populist impulses that made him look to the broadest possible sources of national revolutionary support and directed him from the cities to the countryside. And it was his populist trust in the spontaneous revolutionary energies of the peasant masses that allowed him to develop and pursue the unorthodox strategy of "people's war." Such were some of the essential ingredients in the emergence of a distinctively Chinese Marxist revolutionary mentality that proved instrumental in transforming a "revolutionary situation" into a genuine social revolution with the most momentous historical consequences.

NOTES

1. Cited in Jan Myrdal, *Report from a Chinese Village* (New York: Pantheon, 1965), p. xxvii.

2. Cited in Edgar Snow, *Random Notes on Red China, 1936–1945* (Cambridge, Mass.: Harvard University Press, 1957), pp. 60–61.

3. Anna Louise Strong, *Tomorrow's China* (New York: Committee for a Democratic Far Eastern Policy, 1948), p. 18.

4. The exception, of course, is the revolution led by Castro in Cuba. The case is dubious because a good argument can be made that the Cuban revolution did not become communist until well after Castro had achieved state power.

5. "A Single Spark Can Start a Prairie Fire," in *Selected Works of Mao Tse-tung*, Vol. 1, p. 118.

6. This was the title of an article by Mao published in the summer of 1919. For a translation of extracts from the article, see *The Political Thought of Mao Tse-tung*, edited by Stuart R. Schram, rev. ed. (New York: Praeger, 1963), pp. 105–06.

7. *Ibid.*, p. 106.

Suggestions for Further Reading

GENERAL OR SURVEY WORKS

Boorman, Howard L., and Richard C. Howard. *Biographical Dictionary of Republican China*. 4 vols. Columbia University Press, New York, 1967–1971.

Clubb, O.E. *20th Century China*. Columbia University Press, New York, 1964.

Cressey, George B. *Land of the 500 Million*. McGraw-Hill Book Company, New York, 1955.

Crowley, James B., ed. *Modern East Asia: Essays in Interpretation*. Harcourt Brace Jovanovich, New York, 1970.

de Bary, William Theodore, et al., comp. *Sources of Chinese Tradition*. Columbia University Press, New York, 1960.

Fairbank, John K., Edwin O. Reischauer, and Albert Craig. *East Asia: The Modern Transformation*. Houghton Mifflin Company, Boston, 1965.

Hsu, Immanuel C.Y. *The Rise of Modern China*. Oxford University Press, New York, 1970.

Hu Chang-tu et al. *China: Its People, Its Society, Its Culture*. HRAF Press, New Haven, 1960.

Li Chien-nung. *The Political History of China 1840–1928*. Trans. by Teng Ssu-yu and Jeremy Ingalls. Van Nostrand, Princeton, N.J., 1956.

Teng Ssu-yu and John King Fairbank et al. *China's Response to the West*. Harvard University Press, Cambridge, Mass., 1954; paper: Atheneum.

BACKGROUND TO THE 1911 REVOLUTION

Ayers, William. *Chang Chih-tung and Educational Reform in China*. Harvard University Press, Cambridge, Mass., 1971.

Bland, J.O.P., and E. Backhouse. *China Under the Empress Dowager: Being the History of the Life and Times of Tzu Hsi*. London, 1910.

Cameron, M.E. *The Reform Movement in China, 1898–1912*. Stanford University Press, Stanford, Calif., 1931, reprinted.

Chang Hao. *Liang Ch'i-ch'ao and Intellectual Transition in China, 1890–1907*. Harvard University Press, Cambridge, Mass., 1971.

E-tu Zen Sun. *Chinese Railways and British Interests 1898–1911.* King's Crown Press, Columbia University, 1954.

Feuerwerker, Albert. *China's Early Industrialization: Sheng Hsuan-huai (1844–1916) and Mandarin Enterprise.* Harvard University Press, Cambridge, Mass., 1958.

———. *The Chinese Economy, ca. 1870–1911.* Michigan Papers in Chinese Studies, No. 5. University of Michigan, Center for Chinese Studies, 1969.

Forsythe, Sidney A. *An American Missionary Community in China, 1895–1905.* Harvard University Press, Cambridge, Mass., 1971.

Gasster, Michael. *Chinese Intellectuals and the Revolution of 1911: The Birth of Modern Chinese Radicalism.* University of Washington Press, Seattle, 1969.

Ho Ping-ti. *Studies on the Population of China, 1368–1953.* Harvard University Press, Cambridge, Mass., 1959.

Hou Chi-ming. *Foreign Investment and Economic Development in China 1840–1937.* Harvard University Press, Cambridge, Mass., 1965.

Hsiao, Kung-ch'uan. "K'ang Yu-wei and Confucianism." *Monumenta Serica* XVIII (1959) 96–212.

Hu Sheng. *Imperialism and Chinese Politics.* Foreign Language Press, Peking, 1955.

Langer, W.L. *The Diplomacy of Imperialism.* 2 vols. 2nd ed. Knopf, New York, 1950 (1935).

Lo Jung-pang. *K'ang Yu-wei: A Biography and a Symposium.* University of Arizona Press, Tucson, 1967.

Perkins, Dwight H., with the assistance of Wang Yeh-chien, Kuo-ying Wang Hsiao, and Yung-ming Su. *Agricultural Development in China 1368–1968.* Aldine, Chicago, 1969.

Purcell, Victor. *The Boxer Uprising: A Background Study.* Cambridge University Press, New York, 1963.

Schiffrin, Harold Z. *Sun Yat-sen and the Origins of the Chinese Revolution.* University of California Press, Berkeley, 1968.

Schwartz, Benjamin I. *In Search of Wealth and Power: Yen Fu and the West.* Harvard University Press, Cambridge, Mass., 1964.

Wehrle, Edmund S. *Britain, China, and Antimissionary Riots 1891–1900.* University of Minnesota Press, Minneapolis, 1966.

Wright, Mary C., ed. and introd. by. *China in Revolution: The First Phase, 1900–1913.* Yale University Press, New Haven, 1968.

REVOLUTION IN THOUGHT AND CULTURE

Chow Tse-tsung. *The May Fourth Movement: Intellectual Revolution in Modern China.* Harvard University Press, Cambridge, Mass., 1960.

de Francis, John. *Nationalism and Language Reform in China.* Princeton University Press, Princeton, N.J., 1950.

Grieder, Jerome. *Hu Shih and the Chinese Renaissance: Liberalism in the Chinese Revolution, 1917–1937.* Harvard University Press, Cambridge, Mass., 1970.

Hsia, C.T. *A History of Modern Chinese Fiction 1917–1957.* Yale University Press, New Haven, 1961.

Huang Sung-k'ang. *Lu Hsun and the New Culture Movement of Modern China.* Djambaten, Amsterdam, 1957.

Lang, Olga. *Pa Chin and His Writings: Chinese Youth Between the Two Revolutions.* Harvard University Press, Cambridge, Mass., 1967.

Levenson, Joseph R. *Confucian China and the Modern Fate.* Vols. I, II, III. University of California Press, Berkeley, 1958, 1964, 1965.

Tan, Chester C. *Chinese Political Thought in the Twentieth Century.* Anchor Books, Doubleday & Co., Garden City, N.Y., 1971.

Yang, C.K. *Religion in Chinese Society: A Study of Contemporary Social Functions of Religion and Some of Their Historical Factors.* University of California Press, Berkeley, 1961.

RURAL CHINA

Fei Hsiao-t'ung. *China's Gentry.* University of Chicago Press, Chicago, 1953.

———. *Peasant Life in China: A Field Study of Country Life in the Yangtze Valley.* Dutton, New York, 1939.

Freedman, Maurice. *Chinese Lineage and Society: Fukien and Kwangtung.* Athlone, London, 1966.

Hsu, Francis L.K. *Under the Ancestors' Shadow: Chinese Culture and Personality.* Columbia University Press, New York, 1948.

Lang, Olga. *Chinese Family and Society.* Yale University Press, New Haven, 1946.

Muramatsu Yuji. "A documentary study of Chinese landlordism in the late Ch'ing and the early Republican Kiangnan." *Bulletin of the School of Oriental and African Studies* (University of London) XXIX, part 3, 1966.

Potter, J.M. *Capitalism and the Chinese Peasant: Social and Economic*

Change in a Hong Kong Village. University of California Press, Berkeley, 1968.

Skinner, G.W. "Marketing and Social Structure in Rural China." *Journal of Asian Studies*, 24, Nos. 1, 2, and 3 (November 1964, February and May 1965).

Tawney, R.H. *Land and Labor in China.* Harcourt, Brace, New York, 1932.

THE NATIONALIST REVOLUTION

Chang, Carsun. *The Third Force in China.* Bookman Associates, 1952.

Chang Kia-ngau. *The Inflationary Spiral: The Experience in China, 1939–1950.* John Wiley, New York, 1958.

Chiang Chung-cheng (Chiang Kai-shek). *Soviet Russia in China: A Summing-up at Seventy.* Farrar, Straus and Cudahy, New York, 1957.

Chiang Kai-shek. *China's Destiny.* Macmillan, New York, 1947.

Ch'ien Tuan-sheng. *The Government and Politics of China, 1912–1949.* Harvard University Press, Cambridge, Mass., 1950.

D'Elia, M. *The Triple Demism of Sun Yat-sen.* Franciscan Press, Wuchang, 1931.

Iriye, Akira. *After Imperialism: The Search for a New Order in the Far East 1921–1931.* Harvard University Press, Cambridge, Mass., 1965.

Israel, John. *Student Nationalism in China 1927–1937.* Stanford University Press, Stanford, Calif., 1966.

Pye, Lucian W. *The Spirit of Chinese Politics: A Psycho-cultural Study of the Authority Crisis in Political Development.* M.I.T. Press, Cambridge, Mass., 1968.

Shao Chuan-leng and Norman D. Palmer. *Sun Yat-sen and Communism.* Praeger, New York, 1960.

Young, Arthur N. *China's Wartime Finance and Inflation, 1937–1945.* Harvard University Press, Cambridge, Mass., 1965.

——— (Former Financial Adviser to China). *China's Nation-Building Effort, 1927–1937. The Financial and Economic Record.* Hoover Institution Press, Stanford, Calif., 1971.

CHINESE COMMUNIST MOVEMENT 1921–1949

Barnett, A. Doak. *China on the Eve of Communist Takeover.* Praeger, New York, 1963.

Bianco, Lucien. *Origins of the Chinese Revolution 1915–1949.* Trans.

by Muriel Bell. Stanford University Press, Stanford, Calif., 1971.

Brandt, Conrad. *Stalin's Failure in China 1924–1927.* Harvard University Press, Cambridge, Mass., 1958.

Chang Kuo-t'ao. *The Rise of the Chinese Communist Party 1921–1927. Volume One of the Autobiography of Chang Kuo-t'ao.* University of Kansas Press, Lawrence, 1971.

————. *The Rise of the Communist Party 1928–1938. Volume Two of the Autobiography of Chang Kuo-t'ao.* University of Kansas Press, Lawrence, 1972.

Ch'en, Jerome. *Mao and the Chinese Revolution.* Oxford University Press, New York, 1967.

Franke, Wolfgang. *A Century of Chinese Revolution 1851–1949.* University of South Carolina Press, Columbia, S.C., 1970.

Hinton, William. *Fanshen: A Documentary of Revolution in a Chinese Village.* Monthly Review Press, New York, 1966.

Hsiung, James Chieh. *Ideology and Practice: The Evolution of Chinese Communism.* Praeger, New York, 1970.

Isaacs, Harold. *The Tragedy of the Chinese Revolution.* Stanford University Press, Stanford, Calif., 1951.

Johnson, Chalmers A. *Peasant Nationalism and Communist Power: The Emergence of Revolutionary China, 1937–1945.* Stanford University Press, Stanford, Calif., 1962.

Meisner, Maurice. *Li Ta-chao and the Origins of Chinese Marxism.* Harvard University Press, Cambridge, Mass., 1967.

North, Robert C. *Kuomintang and Chinese Communist Elites.* 2nd ed. Stanford University Press, Stanford, Calif., 1963.

Rue, John E. *Mao Tse-tung in Opposition, 1927–1935.* Stanford University Press, Stanford, Calif., 1966.

Schram, Stuart. *The Political Thought of Mao Tse-tung.* Praeger, New York, 1963.

Schwartz, Benjamin I. *Chinese Communism and the Rise of Mao.* Harvard University Press, Cambridge, Mass., 1951.

Snow, Edgar. *Red Star Over China.* Random House, New York, 1938.

Swarup, Shanti. *A Study of the Chinese Communist Movement 1927–1934.* Clarendon Press, Oxford, 1966.

Thornton, Richard C. *The Comintern and the Chinese Communists 1928–1931.* University of Washington Press, Seattle, 1969.

Whiting, Allen. *Soviet Policies in China 1917–1924.* Columbia University Press, New York, 1954.

Wilson, Dick. *The Long March 1935: The Epic of Chinese Communism's Survival.* Hamish Hamilton, London, 1971.